The Very Stones Cry Out

The Persecuted Church: Pain, Passion and Praise

Caroline Cox and
Benedict Rogers

continuum

Continuum International Publishing Group

The Tower Building	80 Maiden Lane
11 York Road	Suite 704
London	New York
SE1 7NX	NY 10038

www.continuumbooks.com

First published 2011

British Library Cataloguing-in-Publication Data
A catalogue record for this book is available from the British Library.

ISBN: 978-0-8264-4272-7

Typeset by Fakenham Prepress Solutions, Fakenham, Norfolk NR21 8NN
Printed and bound in India

The Very Stones Cry Out

Contents

Acknowledgements

This book would not have been possible without the generous assistance of many people.

First, we wish to pay tribute to the courage of those Christians who themselves face persecution, and yet continue to speak out on behalf of their communities at great risk to themselves. Christians from around the world have assisted us: providing and checking information, verifying facts and, above all, inspiring us with their indomitable faith and radiant love. They include Archbishop Benjamin Kwashi of Jos, Nigeria; Group Captain Cecil Chaudhry (Rtd), Executive Secretary of the All Pakistan Minorities Alliance; Dr. Joseph D'Souza, President of the All India Christian Council; Roshini Wickremesinghe of the National Christian Evangelical Alliance of Sri Lanka; Bob Fu, Director of China Aid Association; Archbishop Pargev Martirosyan of the ancient Armenian land of Artsakh – and many others, some of whose stories are recounted in this book. We are also indebted to several well-respected organisations for invaluable source material, including Aid to the Church in Need, Barnabas Fund, Christian Solidarity Worldwide [CSW], Compass Direct, Elam Ministries, Humanitarian Aid Relief Trust [HART], and Open Doors.

Second, we are very grateful to our guest authors, Canon Andrew White, Jonathan Aitken and Mark Bradley for their chapters, each bringing distinctive insights and inspiration based on their personal experience. We are also deeply indebted to Bishop Michael Nazir-Ali for contributing the Foreword and to Archbishop Benjamin Kwashi for writing the Preface.

Third, we are indebted to the advocacy staff at CSW, particularly Anna-Lee Stangl, David Griffiths, Dr Khataza

Acknowledgements

Gondwe, Julia Evans, Annabelle Bentham and Fleur Brading, for providing valuable background information, checking our draft chapters and making constructive improvements to the text. We are also grateful to CSW and HART for providing many of the photographs in the book.

Finally, we are grateful to Nicola Rusk and the team at Continuum for all their assistance in steering us through the editorial stages and helping to transform our vision into reality and our passion into this book.

Caroline Cox and Benedict Rogers

Preface

I struggle with the issue of suffering under persecution for the sake of the gospel. Quite honestly, I feel crushed and come to the brink of giving up when it seems that the more I pray, the more things get worse. Although even in my position I have had to suffer personal attacks, yet that is not so crushing for me as when I know that someone else is going through some unbearable agony for the sake of the gospel.

In our modern world there has been a development in what we describe as persecution, and there is an evasion of truth in much of the world today where Christians are persecuted. Such situations are sometimes referred to as political violence, ethnic clashes, economic or social misunderstandings. This evasion of truth not only gives cover to the persecutors, but it also increases the suffering of those who are being persecuted for the faith. My heart aches and my appetite disappears whenever I receive information about some Christians somewhere around the world being persecuted for their faith.

Persecution is terrible. I would still love the Lord without persecution, but unfortunately it is an inseparable part of the faith! In most cases persecution serves to sharpen the faith, encourage urgency in carrying out the mission, reminds the believer that he is a pilgrim, and gives wisdom as to how to live wisely here on earth.

Jesus said, 'In the world you have tribulation. But take courage; I have overcome the world' (Jn 16.33). These words of Jesus have been proved true in the lives of thousands upon thousands of Christians throughout the centuries. At various times some have thought that once you give your life to Christ everything changes and you will never again know pain or suffering in this life. That is clearly untrue and it is unbiblical. When you give your life to Christ everything does indeed change, but suffering remains part of the agenda, although now it is with a different vision, a new hope.

Jesus himself knew intense pain and suffering, both physical, mental and spiritual, even to the extent that on the cross he cried out, 'My God, my God, why have you forsaken me!' Out of that suffering, however, came victory, and with victory, glory. Without a death there could be no resurrection! Without Christ's going to the very darkest depths of human suffering in terms of physical pain, of feeling totally misunderstood, deserted by his closest friends, abused, mocked, beaten and tortured and slowly killed – without all that, we would have no hope of salvation; without that there would be no defeat of evil and sin; we would remain enslaved to darkness and death, and in suffering we would have no hope; our faith would be worthless.

Thank God that we *have* a Saviour who is with us! That is what brings light in darkness, hope in desolation, endurance under trial, strength in weakness. It may indeed sometimes seem that God does not hear, does not act, that he has deserted us: those sentiments are all there in the Psalms! But the Psalmist never forgets what God has already done in the past for his forefathers, and in his own life, and so he is prepared to hang on, to learn from the past, to learn in the present, and to move into God's future.

My God, my God, why have you forsaken me? Why are you so far from helping me, from the words of my groaning? O my God I cry by day, but you do not answer; and by night, but find no rest.

YET you are holy ... in you our ancestors trusted; they trusted and were saved.

But I am a worm and no man; scorned by others, and despised by the people ... YET it was you who took me from my mother's womb; you kept me safe on my mother's breast.

(Ps 22.1–3, 6, 9)

✝ The Most Rev. Dr Benjamin A. Kwashi
Archbishop of Jos, Nigeria

Foreword

The world is only now coming to an awareness of the extent of persecution of religious groups, and especially of Christians, that there is in the twenty-first century. For much of this awareness, we are indebted to pioneers and stalwarts like Caroline Cox and Benedict Rogers. Writing of the persecution of Christians, they tell us that no other faith and its followers have suffered as much as Christians have in recent years. What are the reasons for this and what can we do about it?

Christians are persecuted in a variety of situations, whether it is by the Communists in China, a dictator in Eritrea, Hindu nationalists in India or in Islamic countries too numerous to mention by name. Christianity is certainly feared because it is a missionary faith and can bring about a radical change in how people view themselves and those around them. It can provide a critique of social and political systems without, unlike Islam, becoming identified with them. In the context of Islam, it is able to challenge the hegemony of the Islamists and can show people the possibilities of freedom.

In chapter after chapter of this book, we find our perse-cuted brothers and sisters commended for their patience in the most difficult circumstances imaginable. This patience is born of trust in God's overarching and undergirding providence. These people daily experience the miracles of grace in how they are provided for, how their friends and neighbours experience Jesus Christ's saving and healing love and how they are delivered, almost routinely, from deadly danger. How can they not trust such a mighty God, even when they find themselves in a dungeon or staring down the barrel of a gun? The rest of the Church needs contin-ually to learn from these martyrs about prayer, proclamation and perseverance.

The rest of the Church also needs to support these beloved brethren in their danger. It is most important to get behind those agencies that are bringing the plight of the persecuted to our, and the world's, attention. It is necessary to support them in their work of bringing spiritual and material succour to these Christians and churches and to educate us about the crisis the worldwide Church faces today – a crisis full of peril but also full of the promise of what Christ, through his Spirit, is doing in the Church and in the world today. We need to support the persecuted Church with our giving and our going. So many of the stories in this book would simply not have been known if Caroline Cox and her colleagues had not gone to visit those under attack or in prison for their faith. Through petitions, marches and vigils we are to be voices for the voiceless. In keeping them constantly before the throne of grace, we strengthen them and ourselves for the work we all have to do.

There are, of course, serious challenges in what we are being asked to do. Unfriendly regimes, secret police, unjust laws all conspire together to prevent access to our brothers and sisters and to be able to minister to their needs and necessities. In the Western world there is considerable illiteracy about the spiritual issues which underlie the perse-cution of Christians. Politicians are wary that their cause should not undermine trade and good political relations with the concerned regimes. There is a dominant, and quite unjustified, belief amongst the political and diplomatic classes that simply improving the economic situation in countries will ease the cause of fundamental freedoms. This has not happened in many oil-rich countries and in some of today's tiger economies and there is no reason to believe that, on its own, economic prosperity or even democracy will deliver the goods. We need also to entrench a strong sense of liberty in the constitutions and laws of many countries, as well as basic principles such as that of equality before the law. The media also have a part to play. Too often, they either do not understand or simply ignore the dramatic stories that are told within the covers of this book. Are they afraid of a backlash, of spoiling cosy community relations or of being refused access to information themselves? We don't know the whole story but suffice it to say that there is a serious task of education and of motivation that remains to be done. Since the break-up of Yugoslavia and the genocide in Rwanda, the international community has been alert to the necessity of protecting groups of people within a country or region if their life or liberty is threatened by traditional or new adversaries. I believe one of the main tasks of advocacy today is to persuade politicians, diplomats and other civil servants to extend such protection also to religious communities under threat, whether these are Christians in many parts of the world, the Ahmadiyya in Pakistan, the Baha'i in Iran or the Yazīdīs in Iraq. Such protection would mean that nation-states would have to safeguard their basic freedoms and civic rights on pain of sanction from the international community. Rather than spending time on the misleading notion of 'the defamation of religion' and the penalties it should attract, the UN should rather be prioritising, under already existing international law, the prevention of incitement to religious hatred which leads to violence or discrimination and the protection of communities exposed to such hatred.

Under God's mighty hand, the increasing awareness among Christians and churches in the West of persecution elsewhere in the world is, I believe, a preparation for times of hardship, discrimination and, yes, even persecution here. Christians will have to adjust from going generally with the flow of culture to being counter-cultural. In certain circumstances, they will have to learn to say, "We must obey God rather than human beings". They will have to refuse to do what the State commands but which God forbids and to do what God commands but which the State may forbid. We know already that this can entail loss of employment, of membership of professional bodies, of opportunity to serve in public office and a host of other disabilities. Our brothers and sisters, whose stories are so vividly told here, have already blazed a path for us to follow. Their predicament is so much more severe than ours but from them we can learn how to bear our own cross and to follow Jesus.

Let us pray earnestly that when the test comes, we too will not be found wanting, that we too will eagerly confess the faith of Christ crucified and to fight under his banner against the world, the flesh and the devil so that, with them, we too will win that unfading crown with the Lord, the righteous judge, has for all who remain faithful to the end (2Tim 4:8).

✠ The Rt Rev. Michael Nazir-Ali
Former Bishop of Rochester
Lent 2011

Introduction

This book was born in the rubble of a burnt church. Crunching over the blackened bricks, charred wood and splintered glass, with the debris of wilful destruction of bibles, drums and figures from a Christmas nativity crib scattered around, the thought came to one of the authors, Caroline Cox:

> I have done this too often! I have walked through just this same kind of rubble of destroyed churches on countless occasions in many different countries. There is no other faith tradition in the world today which has suffered such widespread and often systematic destruction of its holy places ...

It was in Orissa, India, that this thought came, in the immediate aftermath of religiously motivated violence against Christians. But the broken stones of ruined churches cry out in almost all continents, from Sudan to Burma, from Indonesia to Nigeria, from Cuba to Eritrea and from Iran, Iraq and Egypt to Colombia, China and North Korea. As Caroline Cox has walked through the rubble in many of these countries, so too has Benedict Rogers. The torn down crosses in Chin State, Burma, where Christians have been forced at gun-point to build Buddhist pagodas in their place; a Sunday school meeting in the rubble of a destroyed church in Kesbewa, Sri Lanka; and the desperation of a vulnerable Christian community in the Northwest Frontier Province in Pakistan have all spoken to him in the same way the ruins in Orissa spoke to Caroline Cox.

Literally, physically and metaphorically, whether in the destruction of its buildings, the imprisonment of its pastors, the martyrdom of its saints or the elimination of its public expressions of worship, no other faith tradition in modern

1

times has experienced persecution on the scale, breadth and severity as Christianity.

In 1997, Paul Marshall wrote a seminal book, *Their Blood Cries Out*. With the subtitle *The Worldwide Tragedy of Modern Christians Who Are Dying For Their Faith*, and a strapline across the cover of the book that reads: 'Why it is being ignored, why the silence, what we can do', the book documents the extent of Christian persecution in our world at that time. In the past decade or more, this persecution has increased. It is estimated that at least 250 million Christians now suffer some form of persecution – ranging from intimidation, systematic discrimination and harassment to imprisonment, torture and execution.

One of the most challenging aspects of Paul Marshall's book is the Introduction, which was written by a Jewish scholar, Michael Horowitz. He describes how, as a non-Christian, he was appalled by the extent of persecution of Christians – and even more disturbed by the deafening silence of other Christians. He writes:

> The mounting persecution of Christians eerily parallels the persecution of Jews, my people, during much of Europe's history. The silence and indifference of Western elites to the beatings, looting, torture, jailing, enslavement, murder and even crucifixion of increasingly vulnerable Christian communities further engages my every bone and instinct as a Jew.

Michael Horowitz sounded the trumpet, giving the Church in the free world a 'wake-up' call, reflecting the classic message of Martin Niemöller, a prominent Protestant pastor who opposed the Nazi regime and spent the last seven years of Nazi rule in concentration camps:

> First they came for the Socialists, and I did not speak out – because I was not a Socialist.
>
> Then they came for the Trade Unionists, and I did not speak out – because I was not a Trade Unionist.
>
> Then they came for the Jews, and I did not speak out – because I was not a Jew.

Introduction

Then they came for me – and there was no one left to speak
for me.

Pastor Niemoller was writing about the genocidal policies of
Nazi Germany, but his message has further-reaching implica-
tions. Since the publication of *Their Blood Cries Out*, much
of the Christian Church continues to suffer persecution
and much of the rest of the Christian Church refrains from
engagement with their persecuted brothers and sisters, despite
St Paul's compelling message to the church at Corinth:
'When one part of the Body of Christ suffers, we all suffer.'
(1 Corinthians, Ch. 12, v.26).

Today, in Eritrea, over 3,000 Christians are in prison,
some of them held in shipping containers in a country
where the outside temperature can soar to 50 degrees Celsius
(122 degrees Fahrenheit). Who is praying for them? Who is
protesting?

The failure of Christians who live in freedom and relative
plenty to associate with the persecuted church is deeply
saddening for many reasons.

First, whenever we have the privilege of visiting our
brothers and sisters who are suffering persecution, we are
always humbled by their faith, courage, dignity and miracles
of grace. Through meeting our brothers and sisters enduring
persecution, we ourselves are challenged, because, however
much they are suffering in terms of this world's deprivations
and tribulations, their priority request is always for prayer.
How often in regular church services in the churches in the
West do we hear significant prayers for the persecuted Church?

We could all respond positively, but so often people say
'I never knew about what was happening ...'. This is partly
because of preoccupations which prevent churches in the West
from 'looking out' to the churches on the frontlines of faith
and partly because it is hard to disseminate news of persecution through international media. There often seems to be
unwillingness in the secular media to acknowledge a religious,
and especially Christian, dimension to events which they are
reporting and hence it is hard to spread the news.

Second, when churches that are living in freedom and relative comfort do not look outwards and engage with the persecuted Church, they deny themselves the priceless blessings of being inspired by the witness of the persecuted.

As this book will show, the persecuted Church is full of faith, joy and resilience. The stones in the rubble often resound to the sound of joyful worship. Again and again, as we visit the ruined shell of all that remains of a destroyed church, we find worshippers gathering in the ruins – studying their Bibles and worshipping with more joy and fervour than we often find in churches in the West. Their witness echoes the words of Jesus in Luke's Gospel when He said to the Pharisees, who urged him to rebuke his disciples for loudly and joyfully praising God, 'I tell you … if these were silent, the very stones would cry out' (Luke. Ch. 19. v.40).

So, despite destruction of buildings, the Church survives – and it not only survives: it often grows. There is consistent evidence, over history and today, that the blood of the martyrs is the seed of the Church – and the Church seems, amazingly, to flourish when most under attack.

We also find that our persecuted brothers and sisters humble and inspire us with their radiant love for God and their neighbours, including those who have attacked them, even those who have killed their families and decimated their communities. Instead of seeking retribution, persecuted Christians characteristically demonstrate a persistent commitment to reconciliation which will be demonstrated again and again in this book.

Therefore, the message of the book is not one of gloom and doom. For the 'stones which cry out' are not crying out for retaliation or revenge. They are echoing requests for prayer; they are echoing joyful worship and they stand as witnesses to a Christian Church which grows even in the midst of destruction, which loves, which speaks of forgiveness and which enshrines that peace which this world can neither give nor take away.

A word about the book: it is neither a comprehensive 'encyclopaedia' of contemporary Christian persecution nor an exhaustive account of the situation in the countries from which the pictures and stories come. It is a tribute to the faithfulness, resilience and indomitable love of those whose churches have been destroyed and who live, often at great risk, on the frontlines of faith and freedom.

We are very grateful to our 'guest authors' who have accepted invitations to write chapters on some of the most challenging parts of the world today, based on their own first-hand experience: Canon Andrew White on Iraq and Mark Bradley on Iran. We are also grateful to Jonathan Aitken for contributing an Epilogue challenging the Church in the free world to prayer and action; and to Bishop Michael Nazir-Ali and to Archbishop Benjamin Kwashi for the Foreword and Preface respectively.

Most chapters begin with a story, give an indicative account of the situation in the country concerned, and end with an inspirational message.

It is a privilege to put on record these stories and messages, for they come from people of faith who speak 'de profundis' from the ruins of their churches and the assaults on their communities. They open a window for us, who live in the relative comfort zones of freedom and abundance, into another world. The poet Edwin Muir wrote of the 'two worlds' of the paradise of Eden and of the 'other land' of suffering, terror and grief. In this poem, he describes how those who live in the 'darkened fields' of the 'other lands' can experience blessings which cannot be known in the 'comfort zones' of Eden:

> … Yet still from Eden springs the root
> As clean as on the starting day.
> Time takes the foliage and the fruit
> And burns the archetypal leaf
> To shapes of terror and of grief
> Scattered along the withered way.
> But famished field and blackened tree
> Bear flowers in Eden never known.
> Blossoms of grief and charity
> Bloom in these darkened field alone.

What had Eden ever to say
Of hope and faith and pity and love
Until was buried all its day
And memory found its treasure trove?
Strange blessings never in Paradise
Fall from these beclouded skies'
> Edwin Muir, 'One Foot in Eden', from Collected Poems,
> 1921–1958.

It is our privilege in this book to try to echo the messages of 'hope and faith, pity and love' with which the 'stones cry out' and to honour those who transform persecution into grace and destruction into new life. This book is our tribute to them.

Caroline Cox and Benedict Rogers

Chapter 1
Burma: Mystery Not Misery

In 1993, Pastor Zang Kho Let was arrested by Burma army soldiers, and taken in for interrogation. When his answers failed to satisfy his captors, he was subjected to a cruel and torturous death. 'They cut open his mouth to the neck', it was reported. 'They told him: "We cut open your mouth so that you will no longer preach."'[1]

This incident was at the rare and extreme end of the scale of persecution to which Christians in Burma are subjected. Nevertheless, on a daily basis Christians in Burma face grinding restrictions, discrimination and persecution at the hands of one of the world's worst dictatorships. A military regime which brutally suppresses all its people, particularly those who support the democracy movement or belong to the non-Burman ethnic nationalities, and is influenced by a perverted and distorted form of extreme Burman Buddhist nationalism. The regime, the latest in a succession of military dictatorships to rule Burma since Ne Win seized power in a coup in 1962, has a phrase 'Amyo, Batha, Thatana' which means 'one race, one language, one religion'. This sums up its mentality, which makes it intolerant of non-Burman and non-Buddhist minorities.

Chin State

The persecution of Christians in Burma is most acute in Chin State, in the west of the country bordering India. The Chin people are overwhelmingly Christian, and their faith is integral to their identity. Chin people traditionally built crosses on hilltops and roadsides, as a symbol of their faith. As part of its assault on their identity, the Burma Army has forced Chin people to tear down their crosses, and build

Buddhist pagodas in their place, often compelling them to contribute forced labour, construction materials and money in the process. Today, almost all crosses in Chin State have been destroyed. Chin children have been lured from their families by the regime, with the promise of education, but then placed in Buddhist monasteries. Chin Christian children have had their heads shaved and been forced to become novice Buddhist monks. The authorities warn of three major 'dangers to society', which they term 'ABC' – HIV/AIDS, Hepatitis B and Christianity.[2]

Eastern Burma

In Karen State in eastern Burma, the Burma army is conducting a military campaign against civilians, amounting to war crimes and crimes against humanity. Since 1996, over 3,500 villages have been destroyed. Civilians have been beheaded, severely tortured and mutilated, or shot on sight at point-blank range. Rape and forced labour are widespread and systematic.

Although these atrocities affect all Karen people, Christians, who make up about 40 per cent of the population, are often targeted first. When the Burma army enters a village, they typically burn down the church and often leave the Buddhist monastery standing. Pastors are often among the first victims. For the Karenni people, the majority of whom are Christian, the situation is similar.

Restrictions and discrimination in the cities

In Burma's urban areas Christians may not face physical persecution, and on the surface it would appear that they have freedom to worship. Several church spires can be seen prominently in Rangoon, Burma's largest city, and Sunday services are held with no difficulty. However, under the surface Christians even in the cities are not free. It is almost impossible to obtain permission to build new churches or to renovate or extend existing ones, and it is very difficult to hold church meetings or events other than Sunday services. Christians in government service face discrimination, and are generally unable to gain promotion in the military beyond the rank of Captain, or at most Major.

From time to time, churches in Burma's cities face a crackdown, particularly those church communities which worship in non-traditional buildings, such as apartments or offices. In January 2009, at least 100 churches in Rangoon – amounting to perhaps as many as 80 per cent of the churches in the city – were ordered to stop holding worship services. At least fifty pastors were forced to sign five documents promising to cease church services.[3] Christian-run children's homes were also raided and forced to close. Several churches that did have their own buildings, including three in South Dagon Township, were locked and sealed. In at least one instance, a church's legal registration was revoked.[4]

Some Christians believe that this 2009 crackdown came because churches had been involved in relief efforts for victims of cyclone Nargis, a horrific natural disaster that struck in May 2008. According to Shwekey Hoipang, a Chin pastor now living in exile, the regime does not like the fact that Buddhists received help from churches, as it fears this could lead to conversions and church growth. He claims: 'The regime does not want Buddhists coming in and out of churches. It does not want Christianity to grow in Burma. Ultimately, the regime seeks the destruction of Christianity. This is part of a top-secret plan by the military to stop Christian growth.'[5]

The regime's hostility to Christianity is not, however, 'top-secret'. A document allegedly from the Ministry of Religious Affairs has been widely circulated in recent years, headlined 'Programme to destroy the Christian religion in Burma'. It contains seventeen points, starting with: 'There shall be no home where the Christian religion is practised.'[6] When the report *Carrying the Cross: The Military Regime's Campaign of Restriction, Discrimination and Persecution Against Christians in Burma*, was published by Christian Solidarity

Worldwide in 2007, the regime reacted with fury, running full-page denunciations in the state-run media every day for two weeks. Mass rallies were organized, particularly in Chin State, and church leaders were forced to declare that they had religious freedom and that the report was untrue.

Some church leaders, however, had already spoken out, exposing the regime's lies. On 20 February 2006, six Christian organizations sent a letter to the head of the military regime, Senior General Than Shwe, appealing for an end to the regime's violations of religious freedom. One of the signatories said: 'We simply cannot let things go on without doing anything. This is because Christian associations have been suffering, and we are feeling the pain deep in our hearts. We have been waiting for things to improve but they have only got worse, and this is the only option left to us.'[7]

Despite this, the faith of persecuted Christians in Burma remains strong. The Roman Catholic Archbishop of Rangoon, Charles Bo, says: 'Pray for Burma – Burma needs your prayers. Prayer works. Prayer changes the hearts of man.'

Burma's democracy leader, Nobel Laureate Aung San Suu Kyi, who has spent most of the past two decades under house arrest until her release in November 2010, adds her voice to the requests for prayer. Herself a Buddhist, she once told a Christian missionary that she reads the Bible regularly and that her favourite verse is in St John's Gospel: 'You shall know the truth and the truth shall set you free' (Jn 8.32). She added: 'I know you are a Christian and I know that Christians pray. Burma needs your prayers. Please ask Christians around the world to pray for Burma.'

A beacon of hope and light in the dark situation in Burma is a Karen pastor who runs a Bible school in Mae La refugee camp on the Thailand-Burma border. A theologian and former lecturer at a seminary in Rangoon, Pastor Simon fled to the border after the 1988 democracy uprising, in order to help his people. He writes extraordinary prayers and meditations in English, which is his fifth language. They capture the spirit of his people. His 'Living Testimony' is one inspiring example of how he transforms the experience of exiles in an overcrowded refugee camp, from limitation and despair into hope, purpose and praise:

> They call us displaced people
> But praise God: we are not misplaced.
> They say there is no hope for our future
> But praise God: our future is as bright as the promises of God.
> They say the life of our people is a misery
> But praise God: our life is a mystery.
> For what they say is what they see
> And what they see is temporal.
> But ours is the eternal –
> All because we put ourselves
> In the hands of the God we trust.

Pastor Simon
Mae La Camp, Thailand

Chapter 2

China: Labourers for the Harvest

At 3 a.m. on Sunday, 13 September 2009 a mob of at least 400 people in police uniforms broke into Fushan Church in Linfen, Shanxi province, northern China. A short while later, two shovel loaders ripped apart the church's 'Good News Cloth Shoes Factory'. The machines then tore into the new church building's foundations, and the mob, armed with bricks and various blunt instruments, beat church members who had been sleeping at the site. At least ten Christians were injured, most heavily bleeding, and some were rushed to hospital. Several lost consciousness.

Government officials were among the attackers. The Zhangzhuang town secretary, Gao Xuezhong, was overheard shouting: 'Strike everything; we will pay for it!' Witnesses claim the Vice County Executive, Duan Yumin, was also involved. 'He dashed around madly on the shovel loaders, pushed over the enclosure wall, and tore down the temporary working houses, restrooms and the factory.' Others smashed windows, doors, kitchen utensils, refrigerators and motorcycles, looted the television and other appliances, and stole money, cell phones, books, clothes and even the factory's business licence from the church members. The attack continued for several hours, until just before dawn. The sun rose on a scene of devastation.

As if this assault on a place of worship was not bad enough, local authorities anonymously instructed the local hospital emergency room to refuse blood transfusions and medical treatment for the injured Christians. Two of those most seriously injured had to be transferred with oxygen cylinders to another hospital.

Twelve days later, on 25 September, Pastors Yang Rongli,

Wang Xiaoguang, Yang Xuan, Cui Jiaxing and Zhang Huamei were arrested when they attempted to travel to Beijing to file a complaint about the destruction of their church. Exactly two months after their arrest, they were jailed for 'illegally occupying farming land' and 'disturbing transportation order by gathering masses'. They were given sentences of between three and seven years. Five other church leaders were given two years' re-education through labour.

Such a horrific attack is not common in China, but it is not unheard of. In 2000, a campaign of destruction of churches was unleashed in Wenzhou, known as China's 'Jerusalem' because of its high proportion of Christians. On 12 December 2000 the *Wenzhou Daily* reported that between mid-November and 5 December, a total of 256 house churches were destroyed in one district alone, while thirty-five were banned and seventy-four taken for other purposes. In Changnan county, four churches were destroyed and four seized for other purposes. At least sixty-two anti-religion teams were sent out throughout the four local districts to destroy churches. Twenty-six churches were bombed. The local authorities were open in admitting the attacks, confirming the destruction of hundreds of places of worship. They also declared their intention to demolish illegal religious buildings and 'correct' lifestyles that have become 'decadent' through following unregistered religious groups.

Imprisonment

Over the years, hundreds of Christians have been jailed in China, and once in a while a new crackdown begins, followed by a period of apparent relaxation. On 6 August 2004, for example, more than 100 house church leaders were arrested in Tongxu County, Kaifeng City, Henan Province as they began a two-week retreat. Over 200 military police, Public Security Bureau (PSB) officers and other officials surrounded the venue and dragged the participants away. Three years later, 270 Christian leaders were arrested in Hedeng District,

Linyi City, Shandong Province. In 2008, in the run-up to the Beijing Olympics, twenty-one prominent Christian leaders were sentenced to re-education through labour for terms between fifteen months and three years.

Since 2008 the number of Christians in prison in China appears to have declined, and mass arrests have not occurred. Nevertheless, many remain in jail.

Alimujiang Yimiti

Among the most prominent cases is that of Alimujiang Yimiti (whose Uyghur name is Alimjan Yimit), a Uyghur Christian from Xinjiang Province who was sentenced to fifteen years' imprisonment on 7 November 2009. Accused of 'revealing state secrets to overseas organizations', it is believed that the real reason for his imprisonment is his religious faith.

Alimujiang Yimiti converted from Islam to Christianity in 1995, and this attracted the attention of the authorities. In January 2008 he was arrested, after he had been accused by the local authorities in Kashgar of engaging in unlawful religious infiltrative activities, spreading religious propaganda among the Uyghurs and raising up Christian believers. The charge of 'revealing state secrets to overseas organisations' came after he had talked to an American Christian. The UN Working Group on Arbitrary Detention concluded that his detention is 'arbitrary' and that he is jailed 'solely for his religious faith and religious activities'.

Gao Zhisheng

Christian human rights lawyer Gao Zhisheng is another prominent case for concern. Gao, a self-taught lawyer who passed the bar exam in 1995, attracted attention in 1999 after he won a $100,000 medical malpractice lawsuit. Two years later the Chinese Ministry of Justice named him one of China's top ten lawyers.

However, by 2005 his situation took a turn for the worse when the authorities were angered by Gao's work defending house church Christians and followers of the banned spiritual group Falun Gong. Subjected to repeated arrests, torture and imprisonment, Gao was forced to shut down his legal practice and he resigned from the Communist Party. On 22 December 2006 he was convicted of 'inciting subversion of state power' and given a three-year suspended sentence, one year's deprivation of political rights and five years' probation.

In 2007, after Gao sent an open letter to the US Congress detailing human rights abuses leading up to the Olympic Games, he was arrested and tortured for more than fifty days. His torturers threatened to kill him if he ever revealed the torture, but courageously he wrote an open letter detailing his horrific experience. On 4 February 2009 he was taken away by police from his home in Shaanxi province and disappeared for 400 days. At the end of March 2010, he reappeared briefly before disappearing again. His current whereabouts are unknown.

Gao once predicted that every human rights lawyer in China would one day become a human rights case. He was convinced that if he suffered for standing for truth, people who care about justice would stand with him.

The bookstore owner

A bookstore owner and house church leader in Beijing, Shi Weihan, was jailed on 19 March 2008 for publishing Bibles and other Christian literature, which he distributed without charge. He was accused of 'illegal business operations' and sentenced to three years in prison and a fine of 150,000 yuan ($21,975).

Registration

As in other Communist countries such as Cuba, Vietnam and Laos, the major issue for religious freedom in China relates to the registration of churches. During the days of Mao Zedong, the Chinese Communist Party sought to eradicate the Church, and succeeded at least in terms of removing the Church's visibility. Christians were driven completely underground and had to worship in secrecy and at grave risk, as in North Korea today. Life for most Christians in China today is very different.

Despite this difficult history, Christianity is thriving in China. Precise figures for religious believers in China are impossible to obtain, but estimates of those attending the house churches range from 40 million to over 100 million Christians. In December 2009, the official Chinese newspaper the *People's Daily* reported there were 50 million house church Christians alone. In January 2007 China Aid Association reported that a reliable source had been informed that Mr Ye Xiaowen, the director of the State Administration for Religious Affairs, had stated in two internal meetings at Beijing University and the Chinese Academy of Social Science that there are now 130 million Christians in China, including 20 million Catholics.

Over the past thirty years, space for religion in China has expanded significantly, and continues to do so. There is an officially recognized Protestant church, known as the Three Self Patriotic Movement (TSPM), and although it is controlled by the Chinese Communist Party, many TSPM churches are led by Bible-believing pastors and are filled with Christ-centred worshippers. The Catholic Church experiences a more complex situation, as the Chinese government refuses to accept the authority of the Vatican. The Catholic Patriotic Association (CPA) is the Catholic Church officially recognized by Beijing, but is not linked to Rome. Catholics in communion with Rome worship illegally, and Catholic leaders, priests and bishops face imprisonment as a result, although the Vatican has recognized some CPA Bishops and priests and many CPA worshippers have links to the underground Catholic Church as well. There is far more contact between the registered and unregistered churches, both Protestant and Catholic, than ever before.

The widespread, violent persecution of Christians in

China has diminished in recent years. Mass arrests and the destruction of churches are a rare event today, and unregistered churches that do experience difficulties are more likely to encounter frustrating, bureaucratic restrictions rather than intense and bloody persecution. For example, church leaders have reported being told by the local Committee for Religious Affairs (CRA) that they should keep their meetings to a maximum of 100 people, and that they should not engage in evangelism. Yet churches are in a catch-22 situation – they are illegal if they are not registered, but it has proven almost impossible to register outside the TSPM, although officially the Chinese government claims it can be done. Only two churches are known to have successfully registered outside the TSPM structure, and one of these had its licence revoked a few months later. Many churches have been told by local officials they are not eligible for registration, leaving them in a legal grey area. There are, of course, exceptions, involving severe brutality on the part of the authorities, especially where individuals make political statements or engage in political activity. The general trend is positive, but the plight of individuals such as Gao and Alimujiang proves that there is a long way to go before full religious freedom exists in China.

Conclusion

Whether in periods of intense persecution or frustrating restrictions, Christians in China have displayed extraordinary levels of persistence and determination, grounded in faith, courage and hope. One example is Pastor Zhang Mingxuan, sometimes known as 'Pastor Bike' because he has travelled throughout the country on a bicycle preaching. Despite having been imprisoned twelve times, he has written several open letters to China's leaders and the international community on behalf of the Chinese House Church Alliance, which he leads. Prior to the Beijing Olympics in 2008, Pastor Zhang was arrested for writing an open letter to the international community, in which he detailed his experiences of persecution and called for prayer for China. In his letter to President Hu Jintao, Pastor Zhang described his many experiences of imprisonment, beating and torture, and pleaded for change. He wrote:

> President Hu, the Holy Spirit has moved me to write this following letter to you at 23:00 near midnight. I know you are sitting far away in the Central Party Committee and I would like to know if you know what is going on in the rest of China under your leadership, and if you know the hardship among the common people ... President Hu, are you aware that the officials under you arrest, beat and drive away the Christians from their homes? Our brothers and sisters are being detained because they do not bribe the officials. Do you not think their souls will tell God about their sufferings? ... President Hu, I was selected by God 21 years ago. Belief in Jesus has changed my life ... You are high above there and have you really not heard of these: corruption, bribery, collusion between the officials and the local despots in doing evil deeds, cheating their superiors and covering up from their subordinates and currying favour with their superiors? I implore you to seriously consider the misery of the common people and urge the officials subordinate to you to stop persecuting Christians and implement their promises in the constitution on religious freedom ... President Hu, please forgive me if I offended your dignity. At the time I began to write this open letter to you, I had already fully prepared to die because of this. However, I believe both my life and your heart are in the hands of God Jehovah and He will bring peace both to you and me. Our desire is to win justice for the common people in China so that the Chinese society is full of love and care and that China can become free and prosperous and a real powerful country in the twenty-first century in soul and the social system ... I believe this is also the wish of President Hu. I hereby pray to God to bless you and all the officials in power, to give them more wisdom in ruling China.

In October 2000, 21-year-old Pastor Liu Haitao was beaten to death by the police in Henan province. Before his death, he issued a cri de coeur: 'In this so-called nation of religious freedom, thousands of Christian believers are being persecuted for their faith. They are often arrested without warrant, detained in police detention centres, beaten and then sent to "labour educational camps" ... Some of them are persecuted to death just for being faithful to God.'

Liu had only been a Christian for a year and a half, yet his faith showed a depth of maturity that poses a profound challenge to the Church in the free world. In prison he showed his faith through sharing his meagre food with others. While in detention, he wrote these words:

> By His unlimited great love, the Lord saved me. He leads me to eternal life and entitles me to become a son of God. How can I ignore His salvation and freely accept His grace without doing something for Him in return. More than 90 per cent of people in China don't know God. My heart is broken. If the Lord is going to use me, I am ready to give my life to Him and start the journey of serving Him.

As he died, suffering injuries from torture, as well as denial of medical treatment for kidney disease, he told his mother: 'Mum, I am very happy, I am fine. Mum, just persist in our belief and follow Him to the end. I am going now, Mum. Pray for me.' His final word before he died was a very weak, but unmistakable 'Amen'.

Chapter 3

Colombia: Bullet-Proof Worship

On the evening of 6 September 2009, after a church service in the hamlet of Maranonal, three armed, masked men broke into the home of Rafael Velazquez, Pastor of the Foursquare Gospel Church in Montelibano, Colombia. In front of his wife and six young people from his church, the gunmen opened fire, killing Pastor Velazquez instantly.

This was no isolated incident. On average, between twenty and thirty pastors are killed by guerrillas and paramilitaries each year, and over the previous three years, more than thirty-five pastors in just one area had been assassinated by paramilitary groups. In the previous six months in Cordoba, at least fifteen pastors had received threats.

Ordinary church members have also been targeted. In April 2009, three Christians were murdered in Caqueta. Lida, aged 36, had been a Christian for just one month, and Ineida, aged 38, was in the final stages of pregnancy, when the gunmen came. Lida's husband Enrique had been falsely suspected by guerrillas of being an army informant, and so on that fateful day paramilitaries came to their home and killed Lida and Ineida, who helped the family in the house, in front of Lida's two children. They then went to the rice fields to find Enrique, and shot him dead.

When the bodies were found hours later, Lida's two-year-old son was lying on top of his dead mother, crying. The twelve-year-old daughter was completely traumatized. Today, when the little boy is asked about his mother, he says, 'Mama, bang!' and then falls on the floor. No one had talked about their case until almost a year later, when a CSW team visited the area. They feared retaliation.

Colombia is rarely associated with religious persecution.

Those who know anything about the violent South American nation think of the drug cartels, guerrillas and paramilitary forces and the internal conflict which has lasted almost five decades. It is known as a dangerous country for everyone, but not necessarily specifically for Christians. Indeed, internationally known mega churches in the largest cities, and rapid church growth in recent decades, have given us the false impression that Christians in Colombia are free, and if they do suffer it is because they are caught in the cross-fire. The reality, however, is very different.

Christians targeted, churches closed

While Christians in some parts of the country worship freely, a significant number suffer direct persecution because of their faith. Since 2006 over 200 churches have been forced to close, and church activities are forbidden by the armed groups. Entire Christian communities have been displaced.

One of the primary threats to Christians comes in the five districts in southern Colombia controlled by the largest leftist group, the Fuerzas Armadas Revolucionarios de Colombia – Ejercito del Pueblo, or 'FARC-EP'. In 1998 an area the size of Switzerland was ceded by the president to the FARC-EP, as part of a peace process. The FARC-EP, however, took advantage of their new territory to regroup, recruit and re-arm, and establish a base from which to continue their violent, criminal activities. They perpetrated rampant violations against the local population, and singled out Christians for particular assault. The subsequent Colombian administration instructed the military to re-take the FARC-EP territory, and this has further increased conflict and resulted in more displacement of civilians. At least 4.6 million people are internally displaced in Colombia, the second highest population of internally displaced people in the world.

The anti-Christian agenda of the FARC-EP is clear. In 2007, the guerrilla group ordered the closure of all churches and prohibited any religious meetings across much of Caqueta and Putumayo. Anyone who disobeyed was threatened with death. In one case, the guerrillas threatened to 'burn the church with the Christians inside' if they continued to worship. A Christian couple who hosted nightly worship meetings in their home were told in 2008 that their home would be burned down if they continued.

Conflict of values

The FARC-EP's hostility to Christians stems from a number of factors. First, it is ideological. Christians are accused by the leftist guerrillas of 'exploiting the people' and representing 'imperialist interest'. On 5 July 2007 two evangelical pastors, Joel Cruz, aged 27 and Humberto Mendez, aged 63, were kidnapped, tortured and murdered in Huila. Witnesses say the guerrillas threatened the local population, warning that 'they did not want any evangelicals in the area'. Joel Cruz's widow believes her husband was murdered for his faith.

However there are other factors behind the persecution. The armed groups, both paramilitaries and guerrillas, impose general curfews for security reasons, which affect everyone, and as a result they are suspicious of independent gatherings in areas that they control. They also feel threatened by the Church. The values and beliefs of Christians are in direct conflict with the criminal activities of the different armed groups, and so they believe that by forcing churches to close down and forbidding Christian worship, they can reduce the influence of the Church and strengthen their own authority. Christians tend to wish to maintain neutrality in the conflict between the government and the armed groups, discourage any church members from associating with the armed groups, and in some cases speak out bravely against the injustice wrought on the people by the armed groups. As a result, they incur the hostility of the groups, who require total submission.

These combined factors have led to intense suffering. In June 2007, a pastor in Arauca died after being shot nine times by guerrillas in front of his church. On this occasion the killers were not FARC-EP, but a smaller guerrilla group known as the National Liberation Army or 'ELN'. At least fifty people witnessed the murder, including his wife and three children. They confirmed that he was killed for 'conducting worship services in guerrilla territory'. Another pastor in the same city was killed earlier that year. His 15-year-old son, who witnessed his father's assassination, said that the killers asked his father 'if he didn't know worship was prohibited', before shooting him. In December 2007 in central Colombia, a pastor and his wife had to flee after their names were on a guerrilla hit-list. The reason for the inclusion of their names? 'Preaching about Jesus'.

Faith alive

Yet despite the closure of hundreds of churches and the murder of dozens of Christians, the faith and commitment of the Colombian Church is extraordinary.

Many pastors and Christians continue to worship, despite the threats and risks they face. One pastor in Caqueta remained in the area despite receiving death threats for assisting a displaced woman. The pastor and his wife felt strongly that they should not flee, and until now the threats have not been carried out. 'We didn't think God had brought us to this place to be a military target, but for another purpose,' the pastor, who cannot be named, said. 'We prayed to see what plans God had for us. We fasted and prayed and thank God the guerrillas never carried out their threats.'

Since 2003, several Christian organizations have been working to empower communities to document and report violations of religious freedom in their areas. Despite the risks involved, Christians across the country have been carrying out this important work in a coordinated effort to make their plight known. The Colombian Federation of Evangelical Churches (CEDECOL), for example, established a Commission for Restoration, Life And Peace (CRVP) and, working with a Mennonite human rights organization, Justapaz, they are helping Colombian churches to provide support for victims of human rights violations and to advocate for justice. Their offices have been raided and their personnel threatened, and yet they continue this courageous work.

There have been miracles too. In 2005, a pastor from the Nasa-Paez people group in Cauca was taken from his home by guerrillas. With his family watching 50 metres away, he told the guerrillas to carry out their orders. He promised that although his family was watching, they would not seek revenge. He told his potential killers that he believed God would repay good for good and bad for bad. One of the guerrillas pressed the gun against his ribs – but was unable to pull the trigger. The pastor's life was spared.

The following year, this same pastor and seven others from the local community were told they were under threat for trying to expose corruption. Extraordinarily, instead of keeping quiet, he decided to conduct a survey within the community to find evidence that the local authority was collaborating with the FARC-EP. He walked from village to village carrying out his investigation, and believes he found definite proof that the local authorities were linked to the guerrillas. He has received further threats, but continues to minister and speak out.

Yet another pastor tells of attempts on his life, and narrow escapes. On 21 January 2007, while a pastor in Buenaventura was praying at 6 a.m., two bombs exploded four metres from his house. On 7 February 2010, at a Sunday service, someone shot at him. The pastor saw the bullet hole just a few feet from the pulpit where he was standing. It is believed that he was targeted by the paramilitaries, and this illustrates that Christians face danger from three sides: the FARC-EP and ELN guerrillas, and the paramilitaries.

Conclusion

The wife of a pastor who disappeared in September 2008 received letters from Christians all over the world, and she told CSW just how much these expressions of solidarity mean to her:

> They are a real comfort, a reminder that people are thinking of us and praying for us. Often they would arrive at the right moment – sometimes we would be at the point of despair, and a message would arrive and bring us hope. Even though we couldn't always understand what they said, we would pray for each person who sent us a card or letter by name. Even now sometimes, I will open the box where I keep all the letters and take one out and pray for that person.

This same woman speaks for the faith, hope and love displayed by our brothers and sisters in Colombia in the midst of persecution and suffering. Her husband's fate is unknown, but her faith shines in these words:

> I have come to know a God with whom I am in love. I used to only know God as the King of Kings, the Creator of all things, but now God has conquered my heart. I drink him in every day. For that reason I can laugh, I can smile, I can love. I can tell people how God's love has been for me and that it can be that way for them ... Unfortunately people, even in the church, let us down. But I have learned to depend only on God. When people shut their doors, God opens many more doors for us.

Chapter 4
Cuba: Purified by Fire

The Church of the Apostles stood in the Abel Santamaria neighbourhood of Santiago, Cuba, and was home for 900 worshippers every week. Until, that is, 20 November 2007 when the Cuban authorities launched a massive operation to destroy the church building. Bulldozers, other heavy equipment and helicopters were deployed to raze the church to the ground. At the same time, Pastor Alain Toledano and his family were evicted from their home, which was confiscated along with all their belongings.

This was not the only church to be torn down in Cuba. Seven months later, on 2 June 2008, government officials knocked down all the walls of La Iglesia Bautista de Vicente, a Baptist Church in Ciego de Avila, central Cuba, leaving only the frame standing. The church, which was legally registered, had sought government permission to repair the roof, after one of the supporting beams was damaged. Instead of providing approval, the government imposed a fine, and warned the pastor not to make it a 'problem'. A second fine was imposed, and officials threatened to destroy what little remained of the church. Throughout all this, Pastor Eliecer Dorésca Dictan remained silent.

In both these incidents, however, there was a more positive ending to the story, indicative of the complex picture of religious freedom in Cuba. Pastor Alain Toledo's home and belongings were returned to him, and officials, apparently under instruction from the government in Havana, apologized. In the case of the Baptist Church, four days after destroying it, the authorities returned, cancelled the second fine and told the pastor he could rebuild his church. It is believed that the Cuban government feared the news might leak and affect the European Union's impending review of its Common Position on Cuba.

Subtle, refined repression

Since 2009, conditions for Christians in Cuba appear to have improved in some respects. The Cuban government has embarked on a dialogue with the leadership of the Roman Catholic Church, and has appeared more flexible in registering and legalizing some former unregistered house churches. Catholic and Protestant worship services have now been authorized in prisons, and Christians in jail report being able to possess a Bible. In 2008, for the first time in fifty years, five Catholic bishops celebrated Christmas Mass in Combinado del Este, Cuba's largest prison. These are apparent improvements, but it does not mean an end to the suffering of the Church in Cuba. Church leaders are sceptical about the government's intentions. As one pastor said: 'Religious repression has taken a different form. It is more subtle now and more refined and probably more effective.'

For the time being, the destruction or closure of churches appears to be decreasing, and the authorities are instead targeting church leaders with pressure, although some churches continue to face the threat of closure. State security agents and Cuban Communist Party officials regularly visit leaders of Catholic and Protestant churches, with the objective of intimidating them and letting them know they are under close surveillance. The Cuban Communist Party's Office of Religious Affairs continues to exercise strict control of church activities, refusing permission for some religious activities and denying exit visas for religious leaders with plans to travel overseas.

For some individuals, however, there appears to be no relaxation in the authorities' attitude to religion and indeed, perhaps a hardening of heart. In early 2010 a pastor was severely reprimanded for giving a sermon in which he urged his congregation: 'Don't be like Che [Guevara], be like Christ.' All the other leaders of his denomination, as well as other pastors in the same city, were also reprimanded, even though they had nothing to do with the sermon.

In October 2009, two Baptist pastors in Guantanamo were

arrested and imprisoned. For two weeks they were held in solitary confinement, and their families were given no reason for their detention. After their release, they continue to show signs of trauma.

Imprisonment on trumped up charges

Some Christian leaders are jailed on fabricated criminal charges, designed as a cover for what in reality are religious reasons. On 16 July 2009, Pastor Omar Gude Perez was sentenced to six years and seven months in prison, convicted of the crimes of 'falsification of documents' and 'illicit economic activities,' charges his family and church deny. The prosecution also accused him of 'counter-revolutionary conduct and attitudes'. The real reason for his imprisonment, it is believed, was his involvement in the leadership of a fast-growing independent church movement known as the 'Apostolic Reformation'. The church is not affiliated with the traditional, officially-recognized denominations in Cuba, and that may be why the Cuban government regards it as a threat.

Pastor Gude Perez was first detained on 22 May 2008, and spent fourteen months in prison before his trial. After the court rejected the original charge of 'human trafficking' as baseless, fresh charges were trumped up. In January 2010 he was denied the right to appeal.

In prison, Pastor Gude Perez is kept in a cell containing eight cement bunks, in a row of thirteen cells. Between the eight cellmates, there is one small, open toilet, and a tiny water supply from a small opening in the wall. That trickle of water is the only source for drinking and hygiene for eight men. Poor ventilation and little fresh air make the conditions almost unbearable. The prisoners are allowed one hour outside each day, spending the remaining twenty-three hours a day in their cells.

While Pastor Gude Perez has been able to keep his Bible with him, he has been denied permission to participate in religious services or any religious gatherings in prison, and clergy have not been permitted to visit. His wife is only allowed to visit once every three weeks, and she faces continuing harassment. He has been sick as a result of rotten food in prison, and was denied medical treatment for high blood pressure. In December 2009, he was moved to a maximum security prison and held alongside prisoners serving twenty years or more, without explanation.

Harassment

The Rodriguez family have been subjected to a campaign of harassment which has deployed legal and violent means. Pastor Roberto Rodriguez, aged 70, has spent at least two years under house arrest, accused of 'threatening behaviour', but his trial was continuously delayed. A former National President of the Inter-Denominational Fellowship of Evangelical Pastors and Ministers in Cuba (CIMPEC), the Reverend Rodriguez has been summoned to court hearings four times, but each time the proceedings have been suspended without reason. He finally went on trial in September 2010, and was cleared of all charges.

The family has been forced to move from their home in Placetas, northern Cuba, after intense and prolonged harassment by their neighbours who attacked their house, destroyed their septic tank and cut off the water supply. Local authorities gave the neighbours tacit support, a tactic they often use in order to make life miserable for people they don't like, and the campaign culminated in a physical attack on the Reverend Rodriguez's daughter-in-law, Gilianys Meneses Rodriguez, in public, resulting in her suffering a miscarriage. In a perverse reversal of the rule of law, she was accused of disturbing the public order and fined an equivalent of twice the average monthly salary. Her husband, Pastor Eric Gabriel Rodriguez del Toro, was tried on the same charge as his father, and sentenced to one year's probation.

The Reverend Rodriguez himself is in poor health, and has reportedly lost over thirty pounds in weight. It is believed he was beaten by a local official at the police station.

Why such an intense campaign against him and his family? In September 2008, the Reverend Rodriguez led the CIMPEC's public withdrawal from the Cuban Council of Churches, and published an open letter explaining their reasons. The group claimed that it had been subjected to consistent and illegal interference by the Cuban Council of Churches and government authorities. For the Cuban government, such open criticism and defiance were unacceptable.

Clamp down on house churches

Over the past twenty years, as a result of restrictions on religious freedom and rapid church growth, thousands of unregistered churches have developed. Known loosely as 'house churches', they are gatherings of Christians meeting in family homes and in unoccupied properties. Their size varies greatly, some with just a small group of believers and others with congregations of several hundred. It is unknown how many such churches exist in Cuba, but local church leaders estimate between 10,000 and 15,000 throughout the country. Almost all are operating at great risk, without permission, and many have been forced to close down.

In 2005 new legislation was introduced aimed at clamping down on the house church movement. Similar to regulations in China and Vietnam, Directive 43 and Resolution 46, as they are known, require all house churches to register. Church activities must be supervised by the local authorities, no two churches of the same denomination can exist within two kilometres of each other, and there are detailed restrictions on which rooms of a house can be designated for religious use. Yet even with all these restrictions, those who try to register often face prohibitive challenges in the process, and fail to secure approval.

While many house churches have continued to operate illegally, some have been driven to closure as a result of sustained and highly effective intimidation by the authorities. Following Pope John Paul II's visit to Cuba in 1998, about thirty informal 'Houses of Reflection' were established in one part of Cuba, by Catholic lay leaders. Over the past decade, however, local authorities regularly visited Catholic families and urged them to consider the repercussions for them and their children if they continued to conduct religious activities in their homes. In 2007, the last two remaining Houses of Reflection closed.

Fear and hope

As in China and Vietnam, the picture in Cuba is mixed. As one religious leader told CSW: 'Is there religious freedom in Cuba? There is freedom of worship in Cuba. They want us to keep things within the four walls of the church. But when you talk about the work of the Church outside the physical building, you can see there is freedom of worship but there is no freedom of religion.'

There are exceptions, but only because Christians are becoming bolder and are organizing public events without permission. In some areas the authorities are tolerant, but continue to closely monitor the organizers. In one major city in 2010, churches of all denominations came together to organize a mass Easter procession, without government permission. At least 3,000 people took part, a number virtually unheard of in Cuba. The authorities were shocked and surprised, and extremely unhappy.

In March 2010, Alain Toledano Valiente, the pastor of the church in Santiago that was bulldozed in 2007, sent out an urgent appeal for help. His words combine the mixed feelings of Cuban Christians, and echo the poignant combination of faith and fear which is a daily reality for so many of our brothers and sisters in Christ around the world:

Today, very early in the morning, government agents, including the Chief of the Sector (Chief of Police) for the area, better known as Sorsano, members of the Communist Party and others surrounded the house where we live and where church meetings are held ... They said they were going to tell the police to evict us from the house and to confiscate, once again, all of the goods belonging to the church, and that they were going to deprive us of a place to meet in peace and to worship God.

Conclusion

Yet even in the darkest moments, when gatherings are prohibited and church buildings are destroyed, the Cuban authorities have been unable to eliminate the Church. Pastor Carlos Lamelas spent 126 days in prison, and on his release he wrote these profound, honest and challenging words:

Dearly loved brothers and sisters ... My journey has taught me that although we may believe we have a faith that is perfectly cemented in the Word of God, sometimes it is precisely this which is put to the test ... At times I experienced moments of profound hopelessness. This loss of heart was often my worst tormenter, but little by little the test of fire began to purify me, and the Lord strengthened me and poured out His grace over me each day.

In the beginning I was tortured by thoughts of loneliness, and as I arrived at a moment of emotional crisis, just like the prophet Elijah I asked God to take my life. But He, in His mercy, used the Word of God to nourish me and while I carried out an internal struggle with God, He spoke to me from His Word just as He did with Elijah. He said, 'Get up and eat as you still have a long road before you ... I will ensure that a remnant is preserved.' The next day the head of the guards handed me a number of cards and letters which had been arriving at the Detention Centre. They came from countries on all the continents. I knew then that brothers and sisters who I had never met were praying for me and for my family, and even more, that they were sustaining us with their prayers.

Thus I understood from where the strength came that sustained me in the moments when I began to weaken, and how important it is that Christians intercede without dismaying for those who suffer persecution.

In prison the conflicts went back and forth between my body and my spirit. On one hand, I was arrested because of a government manoeuvre against the churches that didn't submit themselves to its dictates, but on the other hand, I knew that God was in control, and in Him, nothing is without purpose. At the same time, we may rebel against the system, but the voice of the Spirit calls us to seek His sovereign will in the midst of the trial.

It was necessary for me to turn myself over to Him, and to dedicate myself to serving Him from prison, discipling those who shared my cell with me. This also included some of my jailers who confessed that they were the children of Christian parents, and in this way I found the grace and favour of God in the midst of tribulation.

Chapter 5

Egypt: Faith Put to the Test

Early in the morning of 7 January 2010, Coptic Christians around the world were in church, enjoying a celebration of a Christmas Eve mass, according to the Eastern Orthodox calendar. Children were doubtless eagerly awaiting the tender lamb dishes and chocolate treats as part of the traditional Christmas feasts; and adults were rejoicing in the ancient liturgy celebrating the birth of Christ.

But in Naga Hammadi, Upper Egypt, celebration suddenly turned to shock, grief and horror, when six worshippers and a policeman were brutally murdered while leaving church, in a drive-by shooting by three Islamic gunmen who sprayed bullets into the crowd. Images of dead bodies, panic, terror, chaos and screaming mothers were flashed around the world, transforming the peace and joy of the Coptic Christmas celebrations into living nightmares.

The attack was claimed to be in retaliation against an alleged rape of a twelve-year-old Muslim girl by a Christian man – although there has not been enough evidence to convict him. Further tragedy hit when, the day after the attack, thousands of Copts gathered at the mortuary to collect the bodies and to protest against the lack of protection for their community. There, six more Copts were killed in a clash with security forces.

On 8 January, three suspects were arrested but the unrest continued. On 9 January, several Christian homes in nearby villages were torched – and Muslim homes were destroyed in retaliation.[1]

Similar scenes of man-made horror greeted the New Year of 2011 when at least twenty-one people were killed and more than seventy others were injured in an attack, during a New Year's service at the al-Qiddissin (Saints) Church in the northern port city of Alexandria. About 1,000 worshippers were attending the New Year's mass at the church in the Sidi Bechr district of the Mediterranean port city. As the service drew to a close after midnight, a bomb went off in the street outside. 'The last thing I heard was a powerful explosion and then my ears went deaf,' 17-year-old Marco Boutros told the Associated Press from his hospital bed. 'All I could see were body parts scattered all over.'

The Coptic Orthodox church, born in the first century, is one of the oldest in the Christian tradition, owing its origins to St Mark, one of the twelve apostles of Jesus Christ. The term 'Copts' originally referred to Egyptians in general. However, over the centuries, following the Muslim conquest of Egypt, the name became more specifically associated with 'Egyptian Christians'. The Copts continue to be proud of representing the older traditions of pre-Arabic Egypt. Their centre, Alexandria, was crucial, not only to the development of the Christian Church, but also as the transmitter of Greek culture to the Western world.

Now, the Coptic Christian community in Egypt is the largest Christian community in the Middle East, comprising about 10–15 per cent of Egypt's population of just over 80 million. The Coptic Orthodox Church claims to have around ten million members; there are around 300,000 Catholic Christians – Greek, Latin, Coptic and Armenian Catholics; and other religious traditions such as Jews and Baha'is represent less than one per cent of the population. The vast majority of Egyptians are Muslims, predominantly Sunni.[2] Egypt is a member of the United Nations and has ratified or acceded to numerous international conventions as well as the African Charter of Human and Peoples' Rights and the Arab Charter for Human Rights which enshrine principles of fundamental religious freedoms.

Article 2 of the Egyptian Constitution states that 'Islam is the religion of the state and Islamic jurisprudence is the principal source of legislation'. However, Article 40 states that 'all citizens are equal before the law. They have equal public rights and duties without discrimination between them due to race, ethnic origin, language, religion or creed'; Articles 46 and 47 guarantee freedom of belief, practice of religious rites, and freedom of opinion; Article 46 also stipulates that 'the state shall guarantee the freedom of belief and the freedom of practising religion'.

However, only the three 'divinely revealed religions' (Islam, Christianity and Judaism) are acknowledged by the state and therefore protected by the Constitution. Adherents of other religions, such as Baha'is, are not granted such protection.

Despite the rights and protection ostensibly guaranteed by adherence to international conventions and Egypt's own Constitution, non-Muslims suffer in many ways. Apostasy is a very sensitive issue and accusations of apostasy can be levied against three groups:

- Muslims who abandon Islam for another religion.
- Devout or secular Muslims who criticise Islam or Islamic institutions.
- Followers of any creed which promotes a faith which postdates Islam, such as the Baha'is.

While people in all these categories are vulnerable to many forms of intimidation and sanctions, Muslims who convert to Christianity, and their families, are often specifically targeted. Although there is no Egyptian legislation dealing directly with apostasy, converts from Islam are often arrested and charged with damaging national unity and social peace in contempt of religion under Article 98F of the Egyptian Penal Code. They can then be tried before the State Security Court as a threat to national security.

Such converts face many legal sanctions. If still married to a Muslim when converting, they risk having their marriages annulled and losing rights over their children; female apostates lose inheritance rights and are unable to marry within their new faith. The children of convert parents have to attend mandatory Islamic education in schools. Converts are also kept under close security surveillance by the State Security Intelligence Service and many have endured periods of detention during which they suffer a wide range of physical and psychological abuse. Well-documented cases include the arrest of three young male converts to Christianity in 1990 who were detained until July 1991. During detention, they were subjected to repeated torture, including electric shocks, burning with cigarettes, beatings and confinement in cells too small to allow them to lie down. After release, following immense international pressure, they continued to live in Egypt, constantly subject to intimidation and threats to their families.

In 2003, twenty-two converts, and those who assisted them, were arrested; some were tortured and one, Islam Abdul Fathr, died in custody.[3]

The Christian and other non-Muslim communities also suffer many forms of systematic or episodic discrimination, including problems associated with ID cards. For example, while religious converts to Islam can change their official records and ID cards within twenty-four hours, the reverse is almost impossible. Moreover, a non-Muslim identity can bring a host of problems with regard to buying property, opening bank accounts and even freedom to travel. Police and law courts give preferential treatment to Muslims, compared with Christians. Discrimination in employment is reflected in the fact that, although Copts represent about 10 per cent of the Egyptian population, they are severely under-represented in the public sector; it is very difficult for them to participate in local and national politics or to attain any senior posts in the armed or security forces, in the judicial and diplomatic services, or in academic institutions.

In 2007, the UN's International Labour Office published a report demonstrating discrimination in Egypt's schools and colleges: 'One of the most resilient forms of discrimination involves the targeting of Coptics [Christians] in Egypt, who are denied equal access to education and equal opportunities in recruitment and promotion.'[4]

And, always, there is the ever-present threat of communal violence. This is not a new phenomenon. CSW lists some well-documented examples of attacks on Christian communities:

- Between 31 December 1999 and 2 January 2000, twenty-one Christians and one Muslim were killed in the village of El-Kosheh, Sohag Governorate, Upper Egypt. The violence stemmed from a dispute between a Muslim trader and a Christian shop-owner on Friday 31 December. Muslim-owned kiosks and Christian-owned shops were damaged or destroyed that day as the violence escalated. The lone Muslim killed was shot by a stray bullet in a neighbouring village. Nobody claimed that Christians killed him. During the violence, local security forces either stood by or became actively involved in the attacks.
- On 7 November 2003, a group attacked Christian homes and property in the village of Gerza, Al-Ayyat district, injuring five Copts.
- On 14 and 21 October 2005, a Muslim mob in Alexandria attacked St George's Church, along with Christian residences and work places.
- On 14 April 2006, attacks on three different churches in Alexandria killed a Coptic man, 78-year-old Nushi Atta Girgis and injured five others.
- In February 2007, a similar mob attack on Christian shops and residences took place in Upper Egypt, following the rumour of a love affair between a Muslim girl and a Christian man.

The pattern of mob attacks after Friday prayers, ignited by simple street fights or rumours, is not a new phenomenon in Egypt's tense history of communal violence. On 11 May 2007, the imam of a mosque in the village of Bemha, Giza asked his congregation to defend Islam in the face of a rumour that a new church was secretly being built. The mob set seventy houses on fire, looted shops and property and wounded many people.

On 12 June 2007, a simple argument between a Muslim and a Coptic Christian carpenter escalated into a brawl involving passers by and ultimately resulted in an attack on the Holy Virgin's Church in Dekheila. The swift response of the local police prevented the incident from escalating further.

A few days previously, on 8 June 2007 following midday prayers at a mosque, a group of Muslims had attacked seven residences and looted shops in the Christian quarter of Zwyet Abdel-Qader, injuring seven people. The attacks were ignited by a fight the previous night between a 21-year-old Christian truck driver and a young Muslim teenager who did not move out of the way to let the truck pass by.

Youssef Sidhom, editor of the respected Egyptian Coptic newspaper Watani, in his editorial on 10 June 2007 described the situation in Egypt as 'a time bomb that can go off any minute'.

Earlier, in April 2007, Bishop Youhannes Zakaria of Luxor (Thebes of ancient times) had warned that the Brotherhood of Islam, an extremist militant movement, was becoming more influential. Recognizing its growing strength in the polls, the Bishop warned that its rise to power would have disastrous consequences for the Christian population, because of its determination to introduce sharia law and to reduce non-Muslim influences. 'The government is very afraid of the brotherhood ... and is concerned for its own survival.'[5]

There is growing concern that the Egyptian government will become more compromised by attempts at appeasement, more reluctant to pursue justice and to take the necessary steps to prevent further unrest. Too often, if arrests are made, following outbreaks of violence, suspects are acquitted. Alternatively, reconciliation meetings may be instigated, which have proved so ineffective as to be regarded as a mockery. A variation on the theme of unsatisfactory responses has been a tendency to 'explain away' an attack as undertaken by a mentally unstable individual – as happened with the case of the attack on three churches in Alexandria on April 2006.

In the light of this disturbing situation, Magdi Khalil, executive Director of the Middle East Freedom Forum, has argued that 'the lack of an effective social and legal deterrence, the patent absence of a pluralistic societal culture and the indifference of the executive, legislative and judicial powers have all worked to create an environment that breeds violence against the Copts'.

Conclusion

Throughout all these times of trial and tribulation, however, there are examples of a faith and forgiveness which shine like a light in the darkness – a light which the darkness will not extinguish; indeed, which shines all the more brightly because of the darkness.

This is illustrated by a poem written by David Aziz, published in a pamphlet entitled 'The Coptic Christmas Eve Massacre: A Youth Perspective':

Please God be our Guide, You decide,
You are there as I die and as my mother cries,
I was looking forward to the fata,
But now I'm getting colder and wetter,
I lie on this…blood stained road,
With my lifeless body on show,

I wanna be free, I wanna be free,
I wanna be free from this body, ye
I wanna be free, let my spirit roam free,
Lord please receive my spirit from within me,

I am filled with lead but I survive,
And though I am dead I am still alive,
I don't hate those who shot me so please don't be bitter,
'Cos life with Christ is much better.
But this is for the best,
When your faith is put to the test,
But it's all over now and I rest,
I said, it's all over now and I rest,
… I can rest.[6]

Chapter 6

India: Caste and Creed – Complexity and Challenge

In August, 2008 violence erupted in Orissa State. A woman, Suva Simi Nayak, from Tiangia village described how a large mob attacked her village on 24 August, killing five people:

> They cut them to pieces, including the Baptist pastor and the village headman. Two children, aged two to three years old also died. In another incident, the mob caught a man called Samuel and asked him if he was a Christian or a Hindu. He replied 'Please wait for five minutes, then I will tell you.' During that time, he prayed to Christ to forgive them. They saw him praying and cut off his hands while he was at prayer and then killed him. They then threw his mother into a burning house while his daughter managed to run away.

India, with a population of 1.1 billion, has a predominantly Hindu population representing about 80 per cent of the people; approximately 14 per cent are Muslim; Christians and Sikhs account for approximately 2 per cent respectively.

This vast, complex society is also divided on lines of the traditional caste system and the 'outcastes' or 'Dalits', who are the victims of many of the worst human rights violations. Although their condition varies, and some Dalits have been able to advance in society, most are denied opportunities for education or social and economic advancement. Many are therefore forced to do the jobs which no one else will do, such as 'manual scavenging': cleaning human excrement from public toilets by hand. They are vulnerable to trafficking, temple prostitution and other forms of abuse. Many Dalits have converted to other religions, notably Buddhism and Christianity, to try to escape from the caste system – yet even within some parts of the Church the caste system continues and Dalits are not free from discrimination. They may often face religious persecution for leaving Hinduism. Furthermore, when they convert to Christianity or Islam they lose the few benefits to which they are entitled from the State as 'Scheduled Castes'. India has an affirmative action programme to assist Dalits, but it is only applicable to those who remain Hindu, Buddhist or Sikh. Those who become Christian or Muslim are denied all such support.

Throughout much of India, there are dramatic differences of wealth and poverty: it is possible to walk in literally one step from a privileged home or a deluxe hotel onto a pavement teeming with people in extreme poverty – many disabled, many sleeping on the streets. It is estimated that India is home to up to one-third of the world's poorest people.

Heightening inevitable tensions is an active Hindu nationalist movement, which preaches hatred and intolerance against religious minorities. The extremist movement has various guises, represented primarily by the Rashtriya Swayamsevak Sangh (RSS) but supported by the Vishwa Hindu Parishad (VHP) and the VHP's youth wing, the Bajrang Dal, as well as core parts of the major opposition party, the Bharatiya Janata Party (BJP). A philosophy known as 'Hindutva' underpins this, and the Bajrang Dal describes itself as 'Warriors of the Hindutva revolution'. These groups have been responsible, sometimes directly and other times indirectly, for violent attacks on Christians and Muslims.

Although the Constitution guarantees citizens the right to propagate their own religion, 'anti-conversion' laws have been enacted in a number of states. These laws place many obstacles for people wishing to consider conversion to another religion as well as serious punishments including fines and/or imprisonment for anyone found 'guilty of activities related to conversion'. In addition to affecting people engaged in acts of overt evangelism, religious groups involved in charitable and humanitarian activities are also affected. Even if religiously-based charitable work is carried out completely impartially and unconditionally, and no attempt is made to convert recipients, it is often misconstrued by extremists and penalized under anti-conversion laws.

These laws have been driven by the Hindu nationalists, whose understanding of the concept of conversion is very different from our own. They refuse to accept that anyone chooses to convert, and instead hold to the idea that people are converted as a result of some external agency. The laws are therefore intended to prevent people from engaging in the act of converting others, but the legal concept is ill-defined and the penalties may be unjust.

Even though India, which prides itself in being 'the world's largest democracy', provides constitutional guarantees of religious freedom, there have been many attacks on religious minorities over the years. Muslims are actually seen by Hindu nationalists as the first enemy, and have suffered horrific attacks such as the massacre in Gujarat in 2004 when up to 2,000 people were killed. However, Christians are perceived as 'foreign' by Hindu extremists, who are sensitive to perceived evangelism and conversion, and so Christians have also been targets for aggression.

Over recent years, there have been a series of attacks on Christian communities, and there are some indications that these may be escalating. The All India Christian Council documents 248 attacks during the period 2008–2010, but this figure excludes the violence in Karnataka and Orissa. Other organizations have recorded up to 200 incidents per year. Accurate figures are difficult to obtain, but are believed to be several times higher than these, because many cases go unreported due to a lack of awareness on the part of Christians about their basic rights or threats by the police. A report by Christian Solidarity Worldwide (CSW): *India: Communalism, anti-Christian Violence and The Law* details a pattern of religiously-motivated violence. 'The worst case of communal violence faced by Christians in post-independence India took place in Orissa state in 2008, including brutal murders and rapes, widespread destruction of churches and property, and forcible conversions to Hinduism'. During these mass attacks on Christians in Orissa, at least 50,000 people were displaced and 70 people were killed. One displaced man told CSW: 'We are not sure about going back to our village. Maybe this is our fate. We cannot become Hindu and go back.'[1]

Although Orissa is an extreme case, acts of violence on a smaller-scale continue almost daily, and are usually condoned by the Indian authorities and unnoticed by the international community. In 2010, for example, according to CSW, at least 196 incidents of violence against Christians in India were reported, of which 97 were verified. The major affected areas, were:

- **Karnataka**: At least sixty-two incidents of anti-Christian violence were reported, thirty-two of which were verified. This is more than any other state in India.
- **Andhra Pradesh**: At least nineteen incidents in 2010 were reported, sixteen of which were verified. As the fifth largest state in India in area as well as in population, with, according to the 2001 census, 66,500,000 Christians constituting 2.35 per cent, Andhra Pradesh has seen the second highest rate of attack against the Church. Among the tense areas where Christians frequently face difficulties are Mahaboobnagar, Hyderabad, Secunderabad and Ranga Reddy.
- **Chattisgarh**: Christians make up about 1.71 per cent of the population of this state, which witnessed the third highest rate of attack against Christians in 2010. At least twenty incidents were reported, and twelve were verified.
- **Madhya Pradesh**: Often called the Heart of India. Since the Hindu nationalist BJP came to power in December 2003, Christians have suffered increased attacks and concerted efforts to tarnish their image. In 2010, at least eighteen incidents of violence against Christians were reported, although only four were confirmed.
- **Orissa**: In 2010, at least thirteen incidents of violence against Christians were reported, a decrease from the major violence in 2008 and 2009 but nevertheless a sign of continuing tensions.

Conclusion

Despite the suffering and the danger of further violence, the Christian communities maintain an indomitable commitment to remain strong in faith; to resist all threats of further harm; and to refrain from capitulation to pressure.

When a Humanitarian Aid Relief Trust (HART) team visited Kandhamal[2] soon after the horrors of the attacks in August 2008, we met the Catholic Archbishop, Raphael Cheenath of Cuttack-Bhubaneshwar. On that very day, he was going to conduct the funeral of one of his priests, Father Bernard, who had died following a very severe beating during the violence.

The Archbishop received us with sadness, composure and graciousness, in a building festooned with flowers around the pictures of Father Bernard. His message to us was entirely consistent with words he spoke following a previous onslaught of violence against Christians in Orissa in July 2008:

There are about a million Christians in Orissa and the Cross of Christ is firmly planted in this state – no persecution can eliminate it.

Chapter 7

Indonesia: Martyrs and Miracles

On 22 January 1999, in the beautiful town of Ambon, in Indonesia's exotic Spice Islands, a group of about 125 Christian children and teenagers had been enjoying a happy time at a weekend Bible Camp – until Sunday afternoon, when everything changed and the price of faith became martyrdom.

This story was told to Caroline Cox by a young teenager who described, in chilling detail, the death of his best friend, 15-year-old Roy Pontoh:

> The youth group from our church had gone away for a Bible study camping weekend. We were having a very happy time until the terrible moment when a group of Muslim jihad warriors came looking for us. They took my friend Roy aside and one of the jihad warriors asked him, 'Who are you?'
>
> 'I am a soldier of Christ,' Roy replied.
>
> The man who asked the question struck Roy with a machete, almost severing his left arm
>
> The man repeated the question: 'Who are you?'
>
> Again, Roy replied, 'I am one of Christ's soldiers.'
>
> The jihad warrior struck Roy with his machete again, leaving a big gash on Roy's shoulder.
>
> The warrior then asked the question a third time.
>
> Although he was bleeding and in pain, Roy's reply began respectfully, using the kind of courtesy title a boy uses when talking to an older man: 'Uncle – I cannot say anything else – I am a soldier for Christ.'
>
> The next swing of the machete ripped open Roy's stomach. Roy shouted 'Jessuss!' As he fell to his knees, the warrior slit his throat – and Roy died.'

Talking to the best friend of this boy martyr, those of us who heard him speak were deeply humbled – not only by Roy's faithfulness unto death, but also by his friend's demeanour. His face was so serene that we had no doubt that, faced with a similar situation, he would do precisely what his best friend had done. And perhaps the most humbling aspect of all was that it seemed as if this momentous event was no 'big deal': this is the price they may expect to pay for our faith – the child martyrs of our day.[1]

Indonesia has had a turbulent history: colonized by the Dutch in the early seventeenth century and then occupied by Japan from 1942–1945. After the Second World War, the nation was subject to the autocratic rule of President Sukarno and then the comparably dictatorial rule of General Suharto from 1967 until 1998.

The country has since been struggling to develop democracy and civil society, with its first direct presidential election in 2004. The world's largest Muslim-majority nation, with a population of 220 million, has achieved an honourable record of religious freedom, tolerance and political pluralism.

The state's foundational political philosophy is enshrined in the 'Pancasila' with five key principles including: a just and civilized humanity, the unity of the nation, democracy and social justice. Commitment to these founding principles has enabled Indonesia to make significant progress towards democracy, a thriving civil society and one of the highest levels of press freedom in the world.[2] However, a significant threat has emerged in recent years, in the form of militant Islamism, initially from predominantly external sources in the form of Lasker Jihad; more recently from various internal pressures.

Early in 1999, problems began to escalate in some of the areas such as Sulawesi and Maluku (the Spice Islands) where Christians had settled and had been living peaceably with their Muslim neighbours. Tensions had been rising in response to an increase of immigration into some of these areas, leading to pressures on employment, housing and general facilities. Then foreign militants began to arrive in large numbers and began attacks on Christian churches and homes. In the early stages of this unrest, some Muslims rallied to the defence of their Christian neighbours. However, the number of foreigners continued to grow and Lasker Jihad established bases in key places such as Ambon and central Sulawesi.

By 20 June 2000, a BBC report claimed:

> The recent escalation of fighting in Indonesia's Moluccas Islands has been blamed on the arrival of more than 2,000 fighters from the Lasker Jihad. The militants began pouring into the Moluccas in early May after receiving military training at a camp 2,500 km away in Java, where the Lasker Jihad are based. Their leader, Jaffar Umar Thalib, has repeatedly warned that his group will send 10,000 members to the islands to wage a jihad or holy war. Religious fighting has claimed some 3,000 lives in both the Muslim and Christian communities since first erupting in January 1999. Since then Lasker Jihad have been linked to several raids on Christian communities in the north of Halmahera Island, in which at least 200 people may have been killed and many more injured. In each attack, the assailants swooped down from the sea and the mountains in pre-dawn raids. Christian leaders said the attackers came in speedboats and were armed with military issue firearms.

As the violence continued, the toll of dead and injured continued to grow and the numbers fleeing their homes escalated to at least 270,000. Particularly disturbing aspects of the conflict were reports of forced conversions. Barnabas Fund issued a press release on 15 December 2000:

> Indonesian Christians Forced to Convert to Islam or Die! Thousands Forcibly Circumcised: Over 700 Christians are being held in mosques on Keswui Island and are being forced either to convert to Islam or face execution. Some 93 Christians have already been killed and hundreds have been forced to convert. At least 20 have been forcibly circumcised as a sign of their 'conversion'.... The horrific violence began on Tuesday November 28 when four Christian villages came under attack

from Islamic extremists. Eight villagers were killed outright and over 3000 fled into the jungle to hide. However the Islamic raiders chased them through the trees, capturing 700 Christians. stories of indescribable terror and fear are beginning to emerge from the very few Christians who were fortunate enough to escape the island.

However, behind the grim statistics and deeply disturbing accounts lie many happier stories – of events which can be seen as 'miracles of grace'; of people, both Muslim and Christian, deeply committed to peace and reconciliation; and personal stories of courage.

For example, Anis Risameesy, a 38-year-old man from the village of Waai, near Ambon told this story. On 6 July 2000, his village was attacked by jihad warriors and much of the village was destroyed. Many of the villagers fled into hiding in the jungle. Anis stayed behind, with the pastor and one or two other men, to see what would happen. To their dismay, they saw the militants regrouping and starting another attack. The pastor prayed and the men began to hurry to join their community hiding in the jungle. Then to their horror, they realized that some of the jihad warriors were beginning to pursue the villagers. Realizing that it would be impossible for his community, with small children, pregnant women and elderly people, to outrun the attackers, the pastor prayed again. It was about 5.30 p.m. and darkness was setting in. But as the pastor prayed, the dusk was suddenly pierced by a strong light, seen by the 3,000 people hiding in the jungle. And in the light, clearly visible to the pastor and a dozen people nearby, could be seen the figure of Christ, and a voice was heard saying: 'Do not be afraid. I will always be with you. Stand up and walk.'

Then, according to all who witnessed this event, thick cloud descended, cutting off the path of the pursuing attackers; but the bright light never stopped irradiating the path for the fleeing villagers. This illumination enabled them to complete the journey through the jungle to their destination at Passo, in a mere thirty-six hours, instead of the four days it would normally have taken. Anis concluded his account of this event: 'It was as if a huge flash-light was covering us as we made our way. We felt amazed and very blessed. We knew that God wanted us to be His witnesses, so we decided to tell the whole world about the miracle we had experienced.'

Caroline Cox visited these villagers in the safe haven where they were living, following their escape, and saw the huge billboard they had painted to commemorate their escape, in thanksgiving to God for His divine protection. And Anis added his belief that the visit of foreigners was an additional blessing: 'I think this interview itself is a miracle! There is no way I could go around the world to tell what happened. But God sent you here, so now we can spread the story of the miracle through you!'

As already emphasized, Indonesia has a well-respected tradition of religious tolerance, and throughout the conflict, which cost thousands of lives, there were many Muslims who also suffered and many who did not want the war. By 2004, the traditional Muslim community leaders in Ambon, together with the Protestant and Roman Catholic leaders, were yearning for a means whereby the violence could be halted and a process of reconciliation could be initiated.

However, the Lasker jihad militants did not want peace and turned their aggression on these peaceable Muslims. Therefore, it was decided to create an organization in Jakarta – well away from the conflict zone. Caroline Cox and her colleagues from CSW were privileged to help to establish the International Islamic Christian Organisation for Reconciliation and Reconstruction (IICORR), with former President of Indonesia, the late Abdurrahman Wahid, as honorary President. The organization's objectives were: to provide humanitarian assistance to those suffering from sectarian conflict; to encourage the voice of moderation and cooperation between both communities; to promote positive relationships between Muslim and Christian communities in conflict areas; to assist in the reconstruction of the social infrastructure, including the rebuilding of places of worship, schools, homes, hospitals and community centres; to facilitate settlement of persons who had been displaced; and to provide educational materials to promote understanding of the beliefs, values and practices of other faiths. Underpinning all the objectives was a realization that reconciliation and reconstruction need to go hand in hand. For reconciliation without reconstruction can leave communities with destroyed infrastructure, unemployment, poverty and a sense of hopelessness – fuelling frustration and the risk of renewed violence. And reconstruction without reconciliation risks renewed violence, destroying such reconstruction as has been achieved – and the situation deteriorates into a downward spiral of anger and potential retaliation.

In 2004, under the auspices of IICORR, the British government funded an interfaith delegation of Catholic, Protestant and Muslim local leaders from the Moluccas to visit Britain. They worked on policies to promote reconciliation and reconstruction. After their return home, when incipient conflict began to erupt again, it was quickly controlled, because of the 'good faith' which had been established under the auspices of this IICORR initiative.

The participants required courage to be associated with this development. One of the Muslim leaders, Mr Elvy, told Caroline Cox, with tears in his eyes, how his daughter had said to him, before attending one of the reconciliation meetings: 'If you go to that meeting, Daddy, and they kill you, I will be proud of you.'

At the launch of IICORR in Jakarta, former (now late) President Wahid, as President of IICORR, emphasized the need for moderation in Islam. In January 2006, he concluded a profoundly significant article in the Wall Street Journal with this plea to his Muslim co-religionists:

Muslims themselves can and must propagate an understanding of the 'right' Islam, and thereby discredit extremist ideology. Yet to accomplish this task requires the understanding and support of like-minded individuals, organisations and governments throughout the world. Our goal must be to illuminate the hearts and minds of humanity, and offer a compelling alternate vision of Islam, one that banishes the fanatical ideology of hatred to the darkness from which it emerged.[3]

But despite such influential voices for peace, violence has continued to plague Indonesia, albeit at a lesser level than the height of the conflict in the Moluccas and Sulawesi at the turn of the century. According to some reports, there have been at least thirty attacks on Christian churches and church property between January 2009 and May 2010 as well as several attempts to revoke church licences. The Jakarta Christian Communications Forum states that at least twenty incidents were reported between January and July 2010,[4] even in Jakarta itself. For example:

> A Catholic church in Kali Deras, Jakarta, had been granted a licence to construct a church building. But on 12th March 2010, a radical Muslim cleric closed the road to the site – and the police took no action. On 27th April 2010, hundreds of Muslims attacked a construction project in Cibeureum village, Bogor district, burned down three buildings and set two cars on fire … The buildings belonged to a Protestant educational institution. On 7th May 2010 a Catholic school in Jatibening, Bekasi, was attacked. Churches in Bekasi and Bogor are facing continuous harassment and threats, and churches in Karawang, Purwakarta, Cirebon and Tangerang have also been attacked.[5]

West Papua is a cause for particular concern. Traditionally, the majority population was Christian. However, recent mass immigration is changing the demographic structure and is associated with tensions arising from competition for jobs and amenities as well as fears of Islamization as Muslims now outnumber the indigenous Christian population in many parts of West Papua, especially the towns. There have been numerous reports of grave violations of human rights and neither international media nor aid organizations are allowed free access. Other serious concerns include: the treatment of political prisoners; environmental exploitation by foreigners; environmental degradation; and serious lack of investment in education or health services.

Amid these continuing problems, with their threats to peace and stability for the affected areas – and, over time, possibly for Indonesia itself – there are positive initiatives to promote peace and reconciliation, reflecting the spirit of IICORR. A number of dedicated Muslim civil society organizations are committed to countering extremism, promoting a moderate, progressive interpretation of Islam and defending religious pluralism and freedom. They include the Wahid Institute, the Maarif Institute, the Liberal Islam Network and the International Centre for Islam and Pluralism. In 2006, the Islamic State University in Jakarta invited Caroline Cox to an interfaith dialogue with participants from Buddhist, Confucian, Hindu and Christian faith traditions, to seek to develop curricula for religious education in the schools designed to promote mutual understanding of the different faiths. There are also a number of inter-faith dialogues promoted by Muslims and Christians.

If Indonesia proves it is able to withstand the threat from militant extremists and to protect the fundamental freedoms of all its citizens, it will continue to earn respect from the international community and could be celebrated as an inspirational example of a truly democratic, tolerant, pluralist Muslim-majority nation.

Conclusion

The commitment to tolerance and reconciliation has been demonstrated by many individual Indonesians, sometimes at great cost.

Pastor Rinaldy Damanik is one of these. During the violence in Sulawesi, he frequently risked his life rescuing and evacuating villagers under attack. He was also involved in attempts to promote peace – but, in such situations, there are those who do not want peace. In August 2002, he and his team had been evacuating Christians from a village which had been attacked, when their vehicles were stopped by an angry Muslim mob.

The police arrived and searched the cars. The next day, to everyone's surprise, they announced that they had discovered illegal weapons in Pastor Damanik's car.

He was arrested on 11 September and sent to prison.

As his friends were very anxious about his trial, they were concerned that there should be seen to be international interest in the proceedings. Caroline Cox, as a foreign parliamentarian, was asked to attend. She went to visit Rinaldy Damanik in his prison cell on the eve of the opening of the trial. The prison was depressing: dark and dingy. But the darkness was lit up by Rinaldy's warm, joyful smile, radiating love. He explained that he had been offered freedom, if he would plead guilty but, as he was not guilty, he could not accept liberty on a false premise.

The next morning, Caroline Cox and her colleagues sat in the front row of the hot, sultry courtroom, facing the three judges seated on a platform. Just a few feet from the visitors, Reverend Damanik stood, alone and defenceless, except for the defence of truth. He addressed the judges:

> Your Honours, I have been offered my freedom, if I will plead guilty. But that I cannot do, because I am not guilty. I cannot accept freedom on the basis of a lie. We cannot build the future, for our children, for our grandchildren, for Indonesia on a lie. Even if I must spend years in prison; even if I must go to the scaffold, I would prefer to go to the scaffold for the truth than to accept freedom for a lie.

Sitting so close to this man who was prepared to accept the scaffold for the truth, the verse of one of Caroline Cox's favourite hymns entered her mind:

> Tho' the cause of evil prosper,
> Yet 'tis truth alone is strong;
> Though her portion be the scaffold,
> And upon the throne be wrong –
> Yet that scaffold sways the future,
> And behind the dim unknown,
> Standeth God, among the shadows,
> Keeping watch above His own.
>
> James Russell Lowell (1819–1891)[6]

Reverend Damanik was given a three-year prison sentence. The next time he and Caroline Cox were to meet was in November 2005. He had been released from prison several months early – he believes it was as a result of prayer and international pressure on the Indonesian authorities. He came to England and visited Caroline in the House of Lords. It was a joyful reunion and he greeted her with the words: 'When you came to that prison it was like a miracle, that someone from the West, a politician, should care enough to come.' But during that happy time together in England they received news which was to transform joy into grief. A few days earlier, on 29 October Islamic militants had beheaded three Christian schoolgirls on their way home from school. Letters were attached to the plastic bags in which their heads were found threatening that a hundred Christian teenagers would be slaughtered – and their heads given as gifts to Reverend Damanik and other Christian leaders.[7]

These threats were not carried out. But the mixture of joy and tragedy is the story of the persecuted church over the ages and in our day.

Reverend Damanik described the comfort he received during his time in prison from the knowledge that he was not forgotten, demonstrated by the letters he received from people all around the world. He kept careful count; 67,985. He likens them to 'a river which came into my cell every day' and they reminded him of this passage from the Book of Isaiah:

For this is what the Lord says:
I will extend peace like a river,
And the wealth of nations like a flooding stream ...
As a mother comforts her child,
So will I comfort you ...

(Isa.12–13)

Chapter 8

Iran: 'We Will Not Deny Our Faith'

Mark Bradley

On the afternoon of 8 August 2009 the harsh voice of a female guard echoed down the corridors of Tehran's Evin prison: 'Maryam Rostampour! Marzieh Esmaeilabad!'

Sitting on their blankets in their cell, the twenty-five other prisoners turned to Maryam and Marzieh. There was friendship in their eyes. After an emotional goodbye, the two Christians were led away by the guard. Inside the cell some of the inmates put their hands up in a gesture of prayer, others wept. They loved Maryam and Marzieh and hoped they would be released. But there was something in the tone of the guard that made them fear.

Maryam and Marzieh were led to a large changing room and ordered to wash and tidy themselves up. Here they learned why they had been called. They were to appear in court the next day. They had been arrested on 5 March and held in Evin since 18 March. From short conversations with their families they knew their case had been so serious the authorities had wanted bail of $400,000 – an impossible figure for an ordinary Iranian family.

From many hours of questioning, some of it blindfolded, they knew their enthusiasm for Christ infuriated their interrogators who thought of them as being 'najess' (unclean) and apostates. So much so that they had both spent more than a week in awful solitary confinement, hemmed in by small two by four meter cells and a silence that suffocated them. Both women had always refused to ever consider renouncing their faith in Christ, but they also vehemently denied any involvement with foreign Christian Zionist groups, an accusation their interrogators always threw at them.

Now they were going to court, but they had no idea what exact charges they would be facing. Would they be charged with being apostates from Islam? Or, worse, would they be accused of being spies? They knew their time in court could literally decide how long they lived for. As they got into the waiting police van, they managed to squeeze each other's hands.

In the drab court room there were not many people. Maryam and Marzieh sat flanked by two female guards. When the three judges walked in, they stood up. It was the deputy prosecutor, Mr Haddad who asked all the questions.

'Maryam Rostampour and Marzieh Esmaeilabad are you Christians?'

The two women prayed silently. Unknown to them hundreds of thousands were praying for them every day as their story was on the internet.

'We love Jesus,' they replied.

'Yes ... but are you Christians?', Mr Haddad repeated his question.

'Yes, we are Christians.'

Mr Haddad raised his eyebrows. 'You were Muslims, and now you have become Christians?'

'We were born into Muslim families,' replied Maryam for both the women.

'So, you are Muslims?'

'No, we were born into Muslim families, but we were not Muslims.'

There is a heavy silence in the courtroom. Both Maryam and Marzieh can hear their hearts beating. They have denied Islam before a Revolutionary Islamic Court. Yet, they also sense a supernatural courage inside them, even a joy they had not previously experienced.

'How can you say you were never Muslims?'

'We were never practising committed Muslims, just Muslims in name like many others.'

Mr Haddad paused. 'Islam is God's perfect religion. It is the last revelation. Do you not feel sad that you do not call yourself Muslim? Do you not feel sad that you now call yourself Christians?'

'We are not at all sorry to be Christians. We love Jesus Christ.' As the women spoke the name of Christ they sensed the authority of the Holy Spirit behind their words and they felt the judges listening, respecting their sincerity.

Mr Haddad drew himself up to his full length and gave an order. 'You must renounce your Christian faith verbally and in written form. You must state before this court that you are not Christians, and then you must write down that statement and sign it.'

Without hesitation both women said: 'We will not deny our faith.'

There was a tense silence. Again the women sensed a silent authority behind their words. The questions continued. Maryam and Marzieh again denied any involvement with politics. They felt the court believed them.

Mr Haddad then came back to the heart of the case, Maryam and Marzieh's faith in Christ.

'How can you believe that Jesus is divine?'

Again it was Maryam who spoke. 'No human can understand who Jesus is. The Holy Spirit, God, must show them. The Holy Spirit showed us who Jesus is.'

Caught off guard, Mr Haddad said without much thought: 'But it is impossible for God to speak to mere humans.'

Maryam swiftly asked: 'Are you questioning whether God is Almighty?'

The court realized that the directness and freshness of the question had unnerved Mr Haddad. He turned to a tired tactic when an argument is lost – personal attack: 'You are not worthy for God to speak to you.'

Marzieh was more than ready for this and gave a reply that left the court in no doubt as to where moral authority lay. 'It is God, and not you, who will determine if I am worthy.'

Mr Haddad could not reply to this. In a tone mixed with religious concern and threat, he brought his questioning to an end. 'I advise this court for you to remain in detention so you can think more and then to inform the court when you have come to a correct decision.'

Maryam replied for them both, 'We have already done our thinking.'

Maryam and Marzieh, committed members of a house church in Tehran, never denied their faith. After 259 days in prison, their only 'crime' being their Christian faith, they were acquitted and have now left Iran.[1] Their case, which attracted worldwide attention, is typical of the intimidation faced by the Church in Iran. Innocent Christians are arbitrarily arrested, their homes searched, personal belongings confiscated, while they are taken to prison for questioning. Some are released the same day, some the next week, others, like Maryam and Marzieh, after months.

Alongside all the harshness of prison, which can include solitary confinement where sometimes the victim is forced to listen to recorded religious teaching all day, there is always the utter uncertainty of what will eventually happen. If their families do make contact with the relevant official, they are usually ordered to pay an exorbitant amount of money so their loved one can be released on bail. Or, worse, there is a wall of official silence – nobody knows anything.

Since 2008 there have been over 300 cases of arbitrary arrest in over 30 cities known to human rights organizations. Given that some church networks prefer not to speak out when their members are taken, it is clear the actual number is considerably higher. Since the arrival of the Islamic Republic in 1979 there have been in excess of a thousand cases of Christians suffering arbitrary arrest and intimidation behind closed doors. Today these are the living stones who cry out for their brothers and sisters in the free world to campaign ceaselessly for religious freedom in Iran.

Ironically the official position of the Islamic Republic is that there is religious freedom in Iran. In Article 13 of the Constitution, Christians, along with Jews and Zoroastrians are specifically mentioned as protected minorities, and to the casual observer this might appear true. Iran's two distinct Christian ethnic minorities, the Armenians and Assyrians, who together number about 250,000, hold services in their own respective languages. As do many Protestant churches – the Anglican, Presbyterian and Assemblies of God.[2]

However in the corridors of power there is a relentless hostility to Christianity. It is rooted in two firmly held beliefs, one religious and the other political.

In terms of religion the leaders of Iran believe Islam is perfect and Mohammad was God's last prophet so all earlier religions and prophets are inferior. For a Muslim to leave Islam and become a Christian insults the glory of Islam. Thus according to both the Koran and the Hadiths, this apostasy is a crime. Hence there is an inherent enmity in the minds of the government towards all Christian churches which hold services in Persian, the mother tongue of the Muslim majority.

In terms of politics, the leaders of the revolution saw the Christian West as generally at war with Islam, and specifically with the Islamic Republic of Iran. Through the Shah and his import of 'shameful' values, the West had sought to undermine Iran's adherence to Islam, but it is believed that this was exposed and triumphantly thwarted by Ayatollah Khomeini; then the West tried to topple the new Islamic regime through Saddam Hussein, but again the soldiers of Khomeini stopped the invaders. Now the new guardians of the revolution led by the Supreme Leader Ayatollah Khamenei and President Ahmadinejad have to deal with what they perceive as more cunning threats – reformers who would let in non-Islamic values through the back door, and the spread of other religions, especially Christianity.

The mindset of the revolution regarding missionary Christianity was bluntly stated by Ayatollah Khomeini. Missionaries were 'agents of imperialism ... with propaganda centres set up for the sole purpose of luring the faithful away from the commandments of Islam.' He then went on to ask: 'Is it not our duty to destroy all these sources of danger to Islam?'[3] This suspicious mentality regarding active Christianity still overshadows the Islamic Republic. Certainly they are religiously motivated to see that Christianity keeps its place as an inferior religion, where weak people who cannot see the glory of Islam must be protected as a 'dhimmitude'.[4] However the hostility that sends out security guards to arrest committed believers is rooted in the fear that Christians pose a threat to the regime, that they could be a fifth column whose loyalty is not with Tehran but with the USA and the West.

This then is the context of intimidation against Christians. To the outside world Iran claims it has a policy of religious toleration, but in reality this only means tolerance for the ancient Assyrian and Armenian churches whose services in their respective languages have no appeal to the Muslim majority. For Persian speaking churches that offer the majority an opportunity to find out about Christianity, there is active hostility.

However this hostility has not resulted in murderous purges of Christians. This is partly because Iranians are not just Muslims, but also children of an ancient civilization that gave the world its first charter of human rights.[5] They are also devotees of their famous poets, such as Hafiz and Saadi. This history generally gives them a more tolerant, and enigmatic view of the world. The average Iranian has little lust for an apostate's blood, whatever their religious traditions might espouse.[6] Another reason is that the government has always had more pressing political priorities than dealing with what, for many senior leaders, is an irritation: that some Iranians are becoming Christian, rather than a serious threat.

Therefore, rather than murderous purges, the hostility of the Islamic Republic to Christianity was first seen in a determination to limit and monitor the activities of the established Persian-speaking churches – the Anglicans, Presbyterians and Assemblies of God – so that the congregations would shrivel and fade away. It appears that the pragmatists of the revolution understood there was a small number of Muslim converts in these different churches and decided to aim at ensuring their numbers declined, rather than providing headlines of the new government executing Christians. Aiming to stop further conversions from Islam, evangelism immediately became illegal; churches were told to keep Muslims away from their services and pastors were asked for lists of their members.

To encourage churches to comply with these demands, it is common for officials to stand outside the entrance of churches during services to monitor attendance and also to attend the service to scrutinize what is being said from the pulpit. Another way of ensuring a church has no effective outreach to Muslims is to ask pastors regularly to report to the Ministry of Information to inform them of all their activities.

When it is deemed necessary, the authorities do not hesitate to arrest any Christians seen to be too active, both to question them and to warn them.

The implementation of this policy has been more severe in the provincial cities where there is no diplomatic community or international press, and it has been generally been successful. In Mashad, Kerman, Shiraz, Isphahan and Tabriz, where the Protestant churches used to have congregations, the churches are now either shut, or the congregations are very small. In Tehran, as already mentioned, the government finds it useful to be able to show that Christian churches are open. However control is very tight, with constant tension between the government wanting to stop the churches associating with Muslims, and the desire of the church leaders to reach out.

One service that always infuriated officials was the Friday Persian-speaking service at the central church of the Assemblies of God in Tehran. It was a very popular service, so much so that there had to be two sittings; the Gospel was preached; and perhaps worst of all for officials, geographically the church is near the university, where on Fridays the Islamic prayer meeting was broadcast to the entire nation. During the 1980s and early 1990s the officials demanded that the church stop this Friday service, but the leaders refused. In the last two years the pressure became so intense that the leaders had no option but to comply. Now the church only has services on Sunday for members.

As well as keeping a close watch on these churches, the government has restricted all wider Christian activities. The

Bible Society was closed in 1990, the printing of all Scriptures and Christian books is illegal and training has been virtually impossible. For a short period one church held night classes, but it was forced to stop. The situation regarding Scriptures and training is not wholly bleak as Elam Ministries,[7] led by Iranians living outside the country, stepped in after 1990 to provide these resources.

Whenever Christians have shown any defiance towards these tight boundaries set by the Islamic Republic, a violent edge to this intimidation appears. One boundary for the zealots of the revolution is that no Muslim convert should ever publicly lead a church. This is too much of an affront for the glory of Islam. The first Muslim convert leader to be murdered in the revolutionary era was Reverend Sayyah in February 1979, the priest of the Anglican Church in Shiraz.[8] His throat was cut. The murderers have never been found. The second was Reverend Soodmand who led the Assemblies of God Ghurch in Mashad. He was warned by the authorities that a religious city like Mashad, home to the shrine of the 8th Imam of Shia Islam, could not tolerate an apostate priest. Though he had the chance to leave, Reverend Soodmand refused. He was hanged in Mashad prison in December 1990. Towards the end of 1993 a court in Sari, in the north of Iran, found the Christian evangelist and pastor Mehdi Dibaj guilty of apostasy and sentenced him to death after keeping him in prison for nine years. An international campaign brought about his release in early 1994, but he was murdered by unknown assailants that summer. In September 1996 Pastor Mohammad Bagher Yousefi, an Assemblies of God pastor from Ghaem Shahr, again in the north of the country, was found hanging from a tree twenty miles from his home. The central church in Tehran refused to confirm this was suicide. On 15 November 2006 the house church leader Pastor Ghorbandordi Tourani was told by religious leaders to return to the faith of his fathers. He refused and on 22 November three men murdered him in the street with knives.

It is not only Muslim converts who have died. Two Armenian Christian leaders, Bishop Haik Hovsepian-Mehr,[9] and Reverend Tateos Michaelian, of the Assemblies of God and Presbyterian churches were also both murdered in 1994. Though the government tried to blame their deaths on the left-wing terrorist organization, the Mujahidin, it is widely thought they were targeted for daring to embarrass the government. Haik Hovsepian-Mehr led the campaign for Mehdi Dibaj's release and Tateos Michaelean publicly denounced Iran's record on religious freedom.

Tertullian's oft quoted words about persecution have certainly proved true in Iran: 'the blood of the martyrs is the seed of the church.' Living stones have been slain, but they have not cried out in vain. When these martyrs began their ministries there were very few Christian converts from Islam in Iran. Now there are thousands, if not hundreds of thousands. For after the murder of Pastor Yousefi, a number of Christian leaders concluded the only way for the Church to function normally was to go underground. There had to be a move away from buildings, to house groups. Here believers could gather much more safely, away from the prying eyes of officials, for worship, teaching and evangelism. The outcome has been that the Church has grown more in the last ten years in Iran than at any time since the arrival of Islam in the seventh century.

As well as the sacrifice of Iranian Christians determined to witness whatever the cost, there is another very simple reason for the growth of the Church: Iranians are open to the Gospel of Jesus Christ. For the experience of the revolutionary government has brought about a serious dislocation in the relationship between Iranians and their national religion. Before the revolution, most Iranians identified themselves with Shia Islam, even if only in a nominal way. Now, after thirty years of war, economic hardship, cultural authoritarianism, and a way of governing that some would call duplicitous, disillusionment has set in. Many are abandoning religion altogether, but atheism does not come naturally to Iranians. So Jesus Christ, long honoured by Iran's revered poets,[10] is the Prophet many want to hear about.

Before the house fellowships, these seekers faced the

daunting prospect of entering a church building, thus advertising their 'flirtation with apostasy'. Now, once believers have confirmed their faith is genuine, they visit an inconspicuous flat where it is easy to feel immediately at home. With a shared sense of ownership, these groups tend to be very committed and motivated, especially in evangelism. One network grew from a handful to over a thousand in several months.

Maryam and Marzieh, and nearly all those detained in recent years have belonged to these house fellowships. As seen, the general pattern has been arrest, detention and exorbitant bail followed, thankfully, by eventual release. For all involved – the arrested believer, their families and the Church – this intimidation is intensely traumatic. The intention of the authorities is to use the arrests to break the will of believers and stop the spread of the Gospel. This is why those arrested are sometimes subjected to solitary confinement in small cells, or worse. It is the hope of the authorities that the believers will renounce their faith in Christ or alternatively, on release, keep quiet or leave the country. Unsurprisingly, this has been known to happen on occasion.

Until very recently the authorities did not publicize these arbitrary arrests of the house church Christians. However, towards the end of 2010 it was clear this policy was changing. At a speech at Qom, the intellectual heart of Shia Islam, the Supreme Leader made a specific reference to house churches as being a cultural threat to the country. In the first week of January 2011 the Governor General of Tehran, Morteza Tamadon, publicly announced the arrest of many Christians calling them 'corrupt', 'deviant' and similar to the Taliban. While it is known that these Christians are ordinary hard working believers, orthodox in their faith, the authorities are deliberately trying to portray them as 'missionaries' and 'hard-liners'. This is an unwelcome development in the policy of the Iranian government towards Christians.

However the overall impression is that despite the constant threat of arrest, the Christians of Iran, living stones indeed, continue to share the Gospel and see their house churches grow. Christians outside Iran cannot stand by their side as they courageously minister: but they can intercede;[11] they can provide Scriptures and other resources; and they can campaign for religious freedom.

Conclusion

This true story brings together the pain of persecution and the openness of all Iranians, even those who work for the security forces.

Sara would never forget the day officials arrived at her home to arrest her husband. She had stood silently weeping as he was handcuffed and led away. After he left, the trauma continued, for the guards started to search the house. As the hands of strangers looked into cupboards and under chairs, opened books and files, she felt violated – and frightened. Would they find their small stock of New Testaments? She felt sick in the pit of her stomach as one of the guards went into their bedroom where they were kept under the bed. She knew he would find them, and a few minutes later he came out with the New Testaments all in a sealed plastic bag. The guard said nothing.

For all the time her husband was imprisoned, Sara worried about the New Testaments. Would they be used as evidence against him? Would they torture him to find out where he got them from? Would they accuse him of being a smuggler? How she wished she had hidden them somewhere else! She was a woman of prayer, and every night she struggled to give this worry to God.

Despite the risk, and the price her family had paid, Sara refused to give up going to her house fellowship. One morning, several months after the ordeal of her husband's arrest was over, she faithfully went to a ladies' morning Bible Study. Here she listened, with increasing excitement, to how a fairly new member of the church had come to faith.

Farzaneh's story began not with her, but with her husband who worked for the police. One morning he was sent to search the house of a 'political' suspect. He found nothing

Abelina, wife of a pastor who was assassinated by an illegal armed group. She, her 13 children (one in the womb) and the entire village were forced to flee after his murder and are now living as IDPs. Photo: CSW

Mirianith who was in her mother Abelina's womb when her father, a pastor, was shot to death by an illegal armed group. Photo: CSW

Two young boys, ages 12 and 13, whose Christian families were killed after they resisted efforts by the ELN to forcibly recruit them – the boys were forced into hiding. Photo: CSW

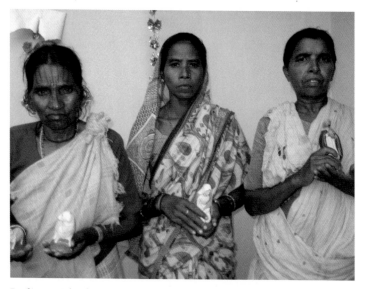

Ladies with destroyed nativity figures, Orissa, India. Photo: Caroline Cox

Broken Body of Christ, Orissa, India. Photo: Caroline Cox

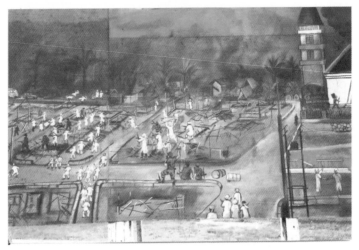

Billboard painting of Jihad attack, Maluku, Indonesia. Photo: Caroline Cox

Revd Damanik, Indonesia. Photo: Caroline Cox

A church in a village to which Christians evicted from their original village had been rehoused. Photo: CSW

St John the Baptist church, Karabakh, framed by the blades of a helicopter during the war. Photo: Caroline Cox

St John the Baptist church, Karabakh, miraculously intact. Photo: Caroline Cox

Bauchi Church, Nigeria. Photo: Caroline Cox

Holy Trinity church, Jos. Photo: Caroline Cox

Holy Trinity church noticeboard, Jos. Photo: Caroline Cox

God still glorified in the ruins of His Church, Nigeria. Photo: Caroline Cox

Russian Orthodox Church in Pyongyang, North Korea.
Photo: Benedict Rogers

A church without a priest: the Catholic Church in Pyongyang.
Photo: Benedict Rogers

Protestant Church in Pyongyang. Photo: Benedict Rogers

Shantinagar, Pakistan after extremists burned down Christian homes and churches. Photo: CSW

The shell of a church in Kesbewa, Sri Lanka. Photo: Benedict Rogers

Sunday school in the ruins of the church in Kesbewa. Photo: Benedict Rogers

Bishop Macram Gassis, Sudan. Photo: Caroline Cox

Boy in burnt church, southern Sudan, 1993. Photo:
Caroline Cox

Hmong church, Northern Vietnam. Photo: Benedict Rogers

Pastor Truong, photographed in November 2009. Photo: Benedict Rogers

God still glorified in the ruins of his Church, Nigeria. Photo: Caroline Cox

Archbishop of Karabakh. Photo: Caroline Cox

Billboard painting of the destruction of a church, Maluku, Indonesia. Photo: Caroline Cox

Burnt Catholic church, Sulawesi, Indonesia, 2000. Photo: Caroline Cox

Shattered dreams for Christian youth in Bauchi. Photo: Caroline Cox

Destroyed cross on burnt church, Orissa, India

suspicious in the home, except fifteen New Testaments in a box under the bed. According to the rules, he knew he had to confiscate them so, while still alone in the bedroom, he carefully put fourteen in marked plastic bags and kept one for himself, which he carefully slipped into his jacket pocket.

For months both he and his wife had talked to each other about Jesus, and had contemplated how to get hold of a copy of the Christian's 'Injil'. Now he had his own copy. When he got home Farzaneh remembered being so excited at finally having a copy of the New Testament in their possession that there was an argument over who would read it first. Eventually they took it in turns, and this was her testimony. Through reading the New Testament she and her policeman husband had come to believe in Jesus Christ. After sharing her story, she held up the same New Testament that had once been hidden under Sara's bed.

Tears poured down Sara's face as she gazed at Farzaneh and the New Testament which had caused her so much anxiety. The memory of that horrendous day, when her privacy was trampled over, drained away as it sank in how great and gracious her Lord was. He truly does work out everything for good.

This story sums up what that is happening in Iran. Yes, there is traumatic persecution. Innocent Christians are suddenly caught up in an opaque and frightening prison system, but in the midst of the pain, the Gospel is spreading.

Background Information on Religion in Iran

- Official state religion: Islam
- Article 4 of the Constitution states that all laws must be based on Islamic principles
- Iran's pre-Islamic religious groups, Zoroastrians, Christians and Jews, are recognized 'protected minorities'
- Population: 67 million
- Religious demographics: 98 per cent Muslim; 2 per cent non-Muslim (including Bahai's, Jews, Christians, Sabean-Mandaeans and Zoroastrians)

- Largest non-Muslim minority: Bahai's: 300,000–350,000
- Number of Christians: estimated 300,000 (majority ethnic Armenians, with some Assyrian Christians and evangelical Protestants).

Source: *US Department of State 2010 Report on International Religious Freedom*

Chapter 9

Iraq: People in The Fire

Canon Andrew White

I was sitting in a conference one day, listening to a man speaking. He was working in Burundi soon after the tragedy that hit that nation and Rwanda. It is not often now that I sit in a conference and listen, but he came out with words I shall never forget. They were true for him then, in his tragedy, and they are true for me now, in the tragedy of Iraq. The words were very simple: 'I only knew Jesus was all I needed when He was all I had left.' My wife was also at the conference and together we have never forgotten that statement. These words are still written in her Bible.

These words are so true for us in Baghdad. As I look around the church, I see so many people and they have all lost so much. Their loved ones are no more, their spouses and their children have been killed in terrible ways. I had just experienced something so terrible in Baghdad, children had been killed in a most terrible way; it was like nothing I had ever seen.

I went from Baghdad to the USA for a friend's wedding. It was a wonderful wedding. But the pain of what had happened in Baghdad was very great and still with me. The next evening, I was preaching at my friend's church in Lexington, Kentucky. I mentioned what had happened in Baghdad and the traumatic way children there were killed. Two people ran out of the church and were physically sick. That night I vowed never to tell people again what happened: the violence and the killing were indeed the worst I had ever seen – but to this day I have never again mentioned it.

I have seen so much brokenness and tragedy here in Iraq – but there is one thing which all Christians in Baghdad agree upon: they have lost so much but they still have Jesus. I am reminded of what St Augustine of Hippo said: 'Christians are an Easter people and our song is "Alleluia".'

We are indeed an Easter people. Like all Easter people, our symbol is the cross. It is a symbol of immense pain and suffering. A symbol of death which we wear around our necks. That which is cruel is often turned into something beautiful. I always wear my Cross of Nails from Coventry Cathedral – the cross made after the bombing of the Cathedral on 14 November 1940. The nails left from the ruins have become a symbol of Easter and reconciliation. It is this Cross of Nails which stands on our altar in Baghdad. It is a replica of this cross which is worn by most of our church community; the crosses are made by church members. So Easter is indeed central to what we believe; also central is the song of Alleluia, which we always sing as we process into church every week.

Not long ago our church was blown up in a bombing and seriously damaged. Our clinic, pharmacy and laboratory were all destroyed. A PowerPoint presentation was made by the Iraqis for our synod. There are pictures before and after the bombing and the restoration. There are no words spoken, just the singing by the choir of one word: 'Alleluia.' We are indeed an Easter people and our song is 'Alleluia'.

Faith does not take away the suffering but it enables us to cope with tragedy. We may have lost everything but we still have Jesus. It is not easy, but we are never on our own. In all our suffering, we are constantly aware of the suffering and the glory of the cross.

Often, in each day, we move from Good Friday to Easter very quickly: the devastation of Good Friday is followed by the glory of resurrection; into the darkness breaks the light of Easter. For us in the fire, tragedy only makes our faith more real. But the pain is still real and we must never forget those who live in the fire. Millions live in Iraq and thousands in our church community. We must never forget their pain and difficulty. I have no regrets that I am called to serve in the fire. I wish my people were not in it – but I have nothing but joy for serving with them. We are in love with each other and the Almighty.

At the same time, our people also have huge needs, which must be met. They need help with medical needs, food and accommodation. The medical and dental needs are met by our large and successful clinic serving up to a hundred people a day from the whole community, not just the Church. Treatment and medicines are free. If people need hospitalization, we have strong links with the private Christian hospital and we pay for their treatment. Needs for food are met with supplies of groceries after church every week. Help with accommodation is very costly: I have to raise $175,000 every month; with God's help I usually manage it.

The key thing is that in tragedy, people need help. Jesus gave us the example: from turning the cheek to giving the coat. We have to show love in action, not just in words. When people ask how they can help, I reply with just two words: 'Prayer and money.'

As I was writing the previous paragraph, I received a message from a pastor in New Jersey, USA. He told me that a nine-year-old girl in his church had been saving to buy a dog. After hearing me preach, she went to the pastor with all the money she had saved, saying she wanted to give it to the children in St George's Church in Baghdad. It is people like this young girl who keep me going and who give us hope.

So we must never forget the people in the fire. Continually, people tell me that we must learn to be self-sufficient and that they cannot continue to help all the time. The fact is, that if we could put out the flames, we would do so, and then we would be able to be self-sufficient. But there is no instant solution. The fire is still raging. As I write, this week several of my people have been killed – which hurts so much. But I know the Lord is with us.

All our people need love. It is love which holds us together – love for God and for each other. We are indeed surrounded by hatred and love holds us together. It is love which is real and radical. We often say that our love has to be as extreme and radical as the hatred and terrorism which we have experienced.

I acknowledge that my experience in the fire is totally different from most people's experience. I also know that I could not minister well in the safety of British or American suburbia.

There, the people need love, too. But having served congregations in normality and in war, I know it is not easy there; it is not. But I love where I am and have no desire to be anywhere else, despite the fact that here there is always pain, terror and total uncertainty. There is no knowing what the next hour will bring, let alone the next day. The only reason I and my people in the Church in Baghdad can cope under fire is because of total trust and faith in the Almighty and our love for Him and one another.

When I think of the Love of God, I always think of a comment by my friend Rodney Howard-Browne. We were talking about the lack of passion of so many preachers. He said they need to see the love of God and he told me that I had seen his love of God in the eyes of children. He was right.

When we talk about love, we are also talking about the possibility of pain – for where there is love, there can always be pain. The source of love may always change or go away. Even in the most loving relationship, ultimately, death will bring separation. But God will never go. He is always there; He is always Love and He is always present.

The fact is that the constant communion with the Almighty, the continual answering of prayer is what gives me certainty. I am surrounded by people who have nothing – which is part of their tragedy. Yet strangely, it is also a means of demonstrating the glory of God. Because our Lord always answers prayers and provides.

In my room in Baghdad, I often watch American Christian TV and hear the message that if you give, you will get. That makes me angry, as my people have nothing to give but their love, and God does give to us and provides for all our needs according to the riches of His glory (Phil. 4.19).

Despite our church being continually under fire, it is the happiest church I have ever served in. We have huge problems but we also have huge joy and a hope based on being the people of faith in a wonderful land of faith. Continually we talk about the role of the land between the rivers – Mesopotamia and Assyria, in the Bible. The land which is the modern-day Iraq is mentioned so often in the Bible. The only land mentioned more often in Israel. Central to all our discussions is the final section of Isaiah Chapter 19 which talks about the highway being built from Assyria (Iraq) to Egypt through Israel. The passage says that Iraq is His handiwork. That gives us so much hope. We do not live in fear because we know that from the beginning (the Garden of Eden was in Iraq) to the end, the Lord is with us and working through Iraqi history. We regularly say that if the world began here, maybe it will end here.

All who could leave have left. Those who had the money to flee have done so – initially to Jordan and Sweden; then when their doors were closed to Iraqis, others went to Lebanon. Now there is nowhere to go. Those who remain in our church are those who do not want to leave. I say that we who are left must stay because we know that God is involved in Iraq and we are part of His story.

However, there is a complex issue regarding theodicy for those living under fire. Many books have been written about how a God of Love can allow such evil. Either He is seen as omniscient and allowing evil or as not being omniscient. At the heart of Christian theology is the belief in a partially inaugurated eschatology. Yet the Kingdom of God is seen as being here and the things of Heaven do indeed happen, but so also do the things of evil. From the time of Resurrection until the Parousia (the second coming of Christ) the Kingdom of God co-exists alongside the Evil Age, in which the Devil has real power and influence and will continue to do so, until Christ returns.

Conclusion

This is the theology which I myself hold to and, I believe, the theology to which Jesus Himself held. Was this not what the Lord's Prayer was in part about when it says: 'Thy will be done on earth as it is in Heaven'? Did Jesus not pray that the Kingdom of God would be manifest in its fullness as it is in Heaven?

So I and many of our leadership team in Iraq see the trauma all around us as the result of the partially inaugurated eschatology and the continuation of the Evil Age. Once again, we return to the issue of love. It is love which gives us hope and purpose, which keeps us together and enables our people to keep on going in the face of tragedy and evil. They see the suffering of Christ in our tragedy but the words of St Thomas Aquinas keep us going. He said: 'It was the love of Christ and not His suffering which was redemptive.' So in our tragedy, when we have lost everything, we do indeed know that Jesus is all we have left – our All in All.

Background Information on Religion in Iran

- Official state religion: Islam
- The Constitution states that no law may be enacted that contradicts the provisions of Islam
- The Constitution does guarantee freedom of thought, conscience and religious belief and practice for all
- Population: approximately 28.9 million
- Religious demographics: 97 per cent Muslim; 3 per cent Christians, Yezidis, Sabean-Mandaeans, Baha'is, Shabaks, Kaka'is, Jews
- Number of Christians: widely recognized that accurate figures are unobtainable, but estimates range from 400,000–600,000. Two-thirds of Christians in Iraq are Chaldeans (an eastern rite of the Catholic Church), one-fifth are Assyrians (Church of the East), and the remainder are Syriacs (Eastern Orthodox), Armenians, Roman Catholic, Anglicans and other Protestants. It is estimated that 50 per cent of the Christian population is located in Baghdad, 30-40 per cent in northern Iraq, and large Christian communities reside in Mosul, Erbil, Dohuk and Kirkuk.
- Key attacks on Christians: in July 2009 six churches were attacked; in February 2010 a wave of killings targeted the Christian community; in November 2010 suicide bombers attacked Our Lady of Salvation Catholic Church in Baghdad, killing at least 42 worshippers.[1]

Source: *US Department of State 2010 Report on International Religious Freedom*

Chapter 10
Laos: Amazing Grace

It was the middle of a Sunday morning worship service on 10 January 2010 when one hundred local officials, police and villagers raided the church in Katin Village, Ta-Oyl District in Laos' Saravan Province. Forty-eight worshippers, including women and children, were rounded up at gun-point, and forced to walk to a field four miles away. Six Christian families' homes in the village were destroyed, and the personal belongings of all eleven families were confiscated. Instead of a home, each family was given a plastic sheet. They were denied food, and came under continuous pressure to renounce their faith.

Almost exactly one month later, the District's Deputy Head came to visit the displaced Christian families, and ordered them to dismantle the temporary shelters they had erected. He told them they could sleep on the ground. Defiantly, the villagers refused, because the children in particular needed shelter. The youngest of the twenty children was just two years old.

Most of these Christians had come to accept the Christian faith in early 2008, after missionaries had visited the area. Their ordeal had begun soon after their conversion. On Sunday 5 July 2009 at 5 p.m., the village chief, elders and local security force broke into the new believers' pig pens and confiscated one pig from each of the nine families, each one worth six weeks' salary. Those who stole the pigs slaughtered them and divided the meat among themselves. The officials told the Christians this was their punishment for disobeying their order forbidding them to believe in Christianity.

A special village meeting was called the next day, at which the local authorities made this announcement:

> Those who follow the Christian faith are practising a foreign religion, not a religion of Laos. We have banned the Christian

faith in our village. Thus, the residents of Katin village should follow only the belief in the spirits, which is considered the Lao religion. If any villager who is found following the Christian faith without renouncing that religion, he or she will no longer be under the official provision and protection of the village.

Harassment continued until and beyond the attack on 10 January 2010. On 15 March 2010 seven of the Christians were summoned to the district office, and told by the district head to reconsider their faith. The Christians refused to renounce their beliefs, and the district head responded by saying he would not tolerate Christianity in his area. They could move, he said, to other districts where religion was tolerated.[1]

Hope mixed with terror

There was a time not so long ago when Christianity was officially 'public enemy number one' in Laos, and Christian pastors were shackled in prison. That was the case up until 2004. Over the past few years, however, the Laotian authorities have typically followed the example of China and Vietnam, and introduced some improvements, opting for more subtle forms of control of religion, in most areas.

Yet incidents such as the one in Katin still occur. For Protestant churches, their legal status depends on which denomination they belong to. Only the Lao Evangelical Church (LEC) and the Seventh Day Adventists are officially recognized under 2002 government decree on religious activity, known as Decree 92. Churches that are not part of these denominations do not find life easy, and the situation shows signs of deteriorating. Since August 2008, the number of Christians in prison has increased, attempted forcible renunciations continue to be reported and forcible evictions of Christians from their villages still occur. Christians are sometimes denied access to education and medical care, on the basis of faith, and from time to time disappearances and abductions happen.

Imprisonment

Some Christians remain in jail, including one Protestant who is serving a fifteen-year prison sentence, believed to be the longest ever imposed in Laos. Mr Tong Chanh, sometimes known as Mr Boon Chanh, is an elderly former government worker from Nonglang village, Sai district in Udomsay province. Arrested on 8 June 1999, he was told his crime was his belief in Jesus and he was accused of 'treason'. Denied food for three days, he was told he was a puppet of the Americans and would have to wait for them to feed him. After three days, officials told him: 'It looks as if America is not coming, so we brothers must feed you.'

On 19 March 2008, eight Khmu Christians were arrested crossing the Meking River to Thailand. They were on their way to attend a Bible training seminar, but had decided to by-pass the check points. They were detained after police found two Bibles, documentation from a Christian group in Thailand and a letter which seriously implicates a local official in the persecution of Christians. They have been held in Udomsay prison since 27 March 2008.

Destruction and displacement

One significant trend in Laos in recent years is the tendency to force Christians out from hostile villages. Once evicted, Christians move to other villages with other Christians, leading to the establishment of large Christian communities.

The Christians from Kok Pho village walked seven hours from Ban Mai Sivanath, having been forced to flee Ban Mai Sivanath, Bolikhamsay district in 2005. Ten families from Nakoon village followed in 2007, walking for eight hours to flee severe harassment. The local authorities had ordered them to renounce their faith or leave the village. When they refused to abandon their faith, they were presented with a deportation order and told there was a policy of 'zero Christians' in the area. Their homes were attacked and stoned, and the wife of a pastor was threatened with death.

In another area, on 9 February 2008 the church in Thong Pan Kham village, Bolikhamsay district was destroyed. A small church with sixteen Christian families and a total of seventy-four people, it posed no threat to anyone, yet local police came to tear it down.

In Hoi Hiep village, Christians sought, and obtained in writing, permission to worship openly in 2007. However, within weeks of receiving permission, the district governor summoned the village heads for a discussion and launched a campaign of harassment of the Christians. Ultimately, the Christians were evicted from the area.

Conclusion

In spite of persecution, severe at times, once again in Laos we see the inspiring spirit of grace among the persecuted Church.

In 2008, dozens of Christians were threatened with expulsion from their homes, and several pastors were arrested. Pastor Sompong Supatto and two other believers were jailed. It was reported that they were held in wooden foot stocks, causing numbness and infection in their legs and feet due to lack of blood circulation.

That same year, raids in three provinces led to the arrest of at least ninety Christians, and it was claimed that several Christian leaders died. One was killed by villagers who poured rice wine down his throat until he drowned. When his relatives buried him and put a wooden cross on his grave, they were accused of 'practising the rituals of the enemies of the state'.[2]

The widow of a murdered church leader has said that she forgives her husband's killers, who tried to destroy their church. The woman, identified simply as Abigail, said: 'Christianity is spreading in Laos – despite persecution – and Christians are growing strong in the faith.' When she preached, the reading was from 1 Corinthians 13: 'Love keeps no record of any wrongs.' She has said that if she were to come face to face with her husband's killer, she would tell him 'about God's love ... even when I do something wrong He always forgives me, so I would tell him I love him, because God loves him, too – and God will forgive him.'[3]

Chapter 11

Nagorno Karabakh: 'We Must Always Love'

High in the mountains of the historic Armenian land of Nagorno Karabakh, stands a magnificent thirteenth century church, dedicated to St John the Baptist. Over the centuries, this has been one of the Armenian Orthodox Church's most holy sites, with a monastery, a university and a seminary.

This is also a place where divine protection seems to have been at work. In 1991, Azerbaijan began to carry out a ruthless policy of attempted ethnic cleansing of the Armenian people from this little land, beginning with 'Operation Ring' – systematic encirclement of Armenian villagers by Azeri troops and forced deportation, with villagers beaten, raped and driven from their homes. Azerbaijan then escalated its offensives, with ground offensives and aerial bombardment.

One of the features of Azerbaijan's assaults on the Armenian peoples was the destruction or desecration of Christian holy places: churches and cemeteries. St John the Baptist Church was a priority target. It was inherently vulnerable: standing on a prominent hillside at Gandzasar, the church is totally defenceless under attack from the air.

Again and again, the SU25 planes flew low over the church, dropping their deadly bombs. Again and again, it seemed as though a protecting arm brushed them aside. The surrounding monastic buildings, some only a few metres from the church, were flattened. But the church remained amazingly intact. And the two shells which penetrated what seemed like a divine protection, never exploded. One remains embedded in the wall, as a reminder, the people believe, of God's divine protection.

Caroline Cox flew over the church many times in helicopters during the war and witnessed the almost unbelievable survival of the church, in the midst of the destruction of the monastic outbuildings.

And there was a blessing, even in the sadness of destruction: beautiful, historic frescoes were discovered in the ruins – exposed by the bomb damage. No one knew they were there; they were a hidden treasure, revealed by the bombs!

There is yet another mystery enshrined in this church. During some of the most difficult days, there appeared one morning, on the walls on either side of the altar, the figures of two angels – faint but clearly discernible. They are certainly not painted by human hands. A confirmation that God's angels are truly protecting this very holy place?

The Armenian people have suffered over the centuries from repeated assaults by many enemies. The land which they owned has shrunk to a mere 10 per cent of former eras. Towards the end of the nineteenth century, Armenians were subject to increasing attacks and pogroms by the Ottomans, with many priests killed and churches destroyed.

Then 1915 saw the beginning of the genocide inflicted by Turkey which culminated in the deaths of one-and-a half million Armenians and the annexation of western Armenia, which is now eastern Turkey.

In 1921, Stalin, with his divide-and-rule tactics, severed part of eastern Armenia and relocated it as the enclave of Nagorno Karabakh inside Azerbaijan. The 1920s also saw the bloody attack on the ancient Armenian city of Shushi by Turks and Azeris, during which they killed 20,000 Armenians, butchered the Armenian Archbishop and impaled his head on a pole. Subsequently, Azerbaijan claimed this as an 'Azeri' town.

With the combination of Azeri rule and domination by the Soviet Union, attempts to crush the Christian faith were doubly ferocious. Churches were systematically destroyed; priests killed or sent to die in the death camps of the Siberian Gulag and Christian activities were prohibited.

With the dissolution of the Soviet Union, Armenia achieved independence and the people of Karabakh began to seek peaceful ways to achieve independence from Azeri domination. Azerbaijan responded initially by threatening to annul Karabakh's autonomous status and rename its capital city with a Turkish name. Then, in 1991, Azerbaijan began a policy of ethnic cleansing through 'Operation Ring' – systematic deportations of Armenian villages, later escalating its assaults into full-scale war on the 150,000 Armenian people living in Karabakh.

During 1991, Caroline Cox accompanied two delegations of independent international experts to the region: one to Armenia; the second to Azerbaijan. The experts came to the unanimous conclusion that Azerbaijan was the aggressor and that its policy of attempted ethnic cleansing of the Armenians from their historic land of Nagorno Karabakh was a gross violation of human rights.

Archbishop Pargev Martirosyan, Primate of Artsakh (the historic name for Karabakh and adjoining Shaumyan) gives this brief historical overview:

'In the fourth century there was the Armenian Catholicos across three regions, and 800 years ago there were around 5,000 churches in Artsakh.

In 1813 the Russians came and they changed our Church's status. There were then only 1,758 functioning churches.

In 1921 there was the double regime pressure from Soviets and Azerbaijanis. We were only allowed 276 priests. In 1930, all churches were closed and all priests were exiled.

In 1989 the Soviets reopened the Diocese after many letters had been written. In November 1989 the Minister of Religion allowed two churches and two monasteries.

To the present day we have forty-one churches and by next year hopefully fifty.

Hundreds of our churches are in ruins or destroyed, with others in bad condition. We would like to restore 200. Azeris also used heavy artillery against the fourth-century monastery at Amaras.

When our people had to flee Shaumyan the Saviour Church was destroyed. Seven people were killed and beheaded, with their heads being thrown onto the altar.

Azerbaijan destroyed our khachkars (stone crosses) and cemeteries in Nakichevan. Recently it was discovered by international media that they destroyed over 5,000 khachkars there. We also found many weapons with writings and inscriptions: "Genocide to Armenians"; "Death to Armenians"; "Happy New Year Armenians".'

In July, 1991, Caroline Cox and a number of colleagues visited one of the villages, Donalar, which had been subject to deportation and she interviewed Azeris (the name often used for the people of Azerbaijan) living in homes which had belonged to Armenians just a few weeks before. At the heart of the village was the shell of the church which had been destroyed by the Azeris when they drove out the Armenian inhabitants. It was being used as a makeshift stable for cows.

In January 1992, when the Azeris escalated their offensives into full-scale military attacks, the 150,000 Armenians living in Karabakh could only defend themselves against seven million-strong Azerbaijan and the well-armed Azeris with hunting rifles against tanks. The capital city, Stepanakert, with a population of a mere 82,000 was subject to constant bombardment from the town of Shushi. Caroline Cox used to count 400 Grad missiles a day fired from Shushi onto Stepanakert and surrounding villages. The inhabitants were confined to basements and cellars, with no light or heat. Besieged, blockaded, bombarded, the people were in a desperate situation. Doctors and nurses caring for the wounded in the hospitals had no anaesthetic or pain-killing drugs.[1]

Then Azerbaijan escalated their attacks with aerial bombardment of Karabakh. Nowhere was safe. The Azeris also used tautology as cluster bombs, scattering attractive metal balls, which children would pick up, with deadly consequences.

The Armenians resisted with grim determination. They had already lost all of western Armenia with the genocide beginning in 1915. They did not want to lose yet more of their historically Christian land, home to some of the oldest churches in the world. The war dragged on, with tragic loss of life for both sides, until a cease-fire was signed on 12 May

1994 – a ceasefire which has remained precariously in place, but accompanied by constant threats from Azerbaijan to renew hostilities with the enormous arsenal of weapons acquired from its rich oil reserves.

One of the most significant developments in the defence of Karabakh was the capture (or liberation) by the Armenians of the hilltop town of Shushi. This had been a famous centre of Armenian culture until 1920 when Turkish forces massacred 20,000 Armenians living there.

The town was subsequently occupied by Azeris who adopted their customary practice of destroying churches. They also drove a road right though the Armenian cemetery, destroying tombstones and ripping open the graves and they tried to blow up the magnificent cathedral. However, this was so well built that it defied destruction. The dome was blown off and glass shattered, but the main structure remained defiantly in place. Therefore, the Azeris, knowing that Armenians would never bomb a church, used the remains of the building to store weapons. So the church was used to store weapons of death, including the massive supply of GRAD missiles which rained down on Stepanakert and neighbouring villages every day. The Armenians knew they could not survive this constant bombardment and that they had to undertake the extremely challenging task of driving the Azeris out of Shushi: a formidable military operation, involving a mountainous assault, climbing steep slopes to attack a very well-defended town.

On 9 May 1992, the attack began. The Armenians feared they might lose a third of their small army – but this was a price they had to be prepared to pay for survival. In the event, they left a corridor open for the Azeris to escape – and after a relatively short but intense engagement, the Azeris fled through the corridor and Shushi was once again in Armenian hands. In stark contrast to Azeri policies, the Armenians were determined to protect the Islamic holy places and placed guards around the mosques to protect them from any damage.

Caroline Cox was able to visit Shushi shortly after these

events and went immediately to the cathedral. Soldiers had taken the now empty boxes which had contained the GRAD missiles out of the church and were sawing them up for firewood. When Caroline entered the ruined church, she was surprised to hear beautiful music: three girls were standing by the damaged altar, singing the beautiful Armenian liturgy. It was an amazing symphony of sound: the combination of the sounds of soldiers sawing boxes which had housed weapons of death and the sound of the girls' clear voices singing the ancient holy music. It was like a symbol of light in darkness; a candle of hope – but was it a candle which would soon be snuffed out? Soon afterwards, a group of retired Turkish army officers came to assist their Azeri friends and the war took a serious turn for the worse for the Armenians. The northern region of Shaumyan was captured by Azeri forces and tens of thousands of Armenians had to flee over the mountains to take refuge in the already devastated little city of Stepanakert.

There were many stories of extreme suffering and also many stories of amazing faith – all the more remarkable, as the inhabitants of Karabakh had not had access to priests, to church worship and, often, not to any Bible, since the combination of Stalinist and Azeri policies had attempted to wipe out Christianity for sixty years.

One story began in the time of deportations. A farmer from the village of Getashen described his experiences. Azeri troops, including the infamous 'Black Beret' Omon Special Forces surrounded the little town with tanks; helicopter gunships hovered overhead. Villagers were rounded up, beaten, and had to watch while their homes were ransacked and their belongings stolen – often accompanied by jeering and taunting. The farmer, knowing the local terrain, managed to escape through the forest and mountains and join the effort to defend his homeland. He described how, after he had escaped, he was shattered by what he had seen happen to his family and his neighbours. Deeply traumatized, he stopped and turned to trees for comfort: it was May, and they were beautiful with blossom. One particularly beautiful tree drew him to it. But as he approached, he saw the body of a five-year-old Armenian girl hanging from a branch – cut in two. He told us how he wept and, in his distress, vowed revenge.

Caroline Cox met him two years later and he entertained her and her colleagues in his makeshift home. Over the simple meal, he stood up to make his welcoming toast, but broke down in tears, saying: 'When we met before, I made a vow to avenge that child's death. But since then, whenever we captured an Azeri village, I could never bring myself to harm a child. So I broke my vow.'

An American colleague at the table stood up and replied: 'Thank you, sir. For the first time in my life, I really understand what it says in the Bible: "Vengeance is mine, saith the Lord." And thank you for the dignity you have shown.' To which the farmer replied, simply: 'Dignity is a crown of thorns.'

A truly profound theology, spoken 'de profundis'.

Conclusion

Archbishop Pargev Martirosyan stayed with his people throughout the dark days of war. Caroline Cox was in Stepanakert on the day on which his house was bombed to smithereens. Visiting him that afternoon in the ruins of his home, she asked if he would like to give a message to the wider world.

This is the message he gave standing in the rubble of his home, during a war inflicted on his people by a nation intent on driving them from their historic land:

> Our nation has again begun to find its faith after seventy years of Soviet Communism and our people are praying in churches, in cellars and on the field of battle, defending the lives of those who are near and dear. It is not only the perpetrators of crime and evil who commit sin, but also those who stand by – seeing and knowing – but who do not condemn it or try to avert it. Blessed are the peacemakers for they will be called sons of God.

Nagorno Karabakh: 'We Must Always Love'

We do not hate – we believe in a God of love. If we want God's victory, we must never hate; we must always love. Even if there are demonic forces at work, not only in this conflict, but in other parts of the world, we must still love – we must always love.'

Chapter 12

Nigeria: Singing in the Ruins

The silhouette of a ruined church stands starkly against the skyline. We are standing in a desolate street in the town of Jos, the capital city of Plateau State in Nigeria, in an area where many of the Christian communities' churches, homes and businesses have been systematically destroyed. As we climb the hill to visit the remains of a burnt Roman Catholic Church, we can hardly believe our ears. For from the empty shell of the church comes the sound of singing and as we enter we find a group of about thirty women praying, singing and engaged in Bible Study.

In front of them, on the remains of the wall behind the place where the high altar would have stood, is a stunning symbol: a blackened shape of a burnt wooden cross with the twisted iron skeleton of the burnt body of Christ still affixed to it.

We introduce ourselves and subsequently enjoy an inspirational time of fellowship and prayer. We depart, with the radiant smiles of these ladies, worshipping and singing in the ruins of their church, indelibly imprinted in our memories.

Nigeria is Africa's most populous nation, with about 150 million citizens. Muslims predominate in the north while Christians form the majority elsewhere, with an estimated 10 per cent adhering to traditional religions across the country.

Much of Nigeria is relatively peaceful and prosperous, although there are intransigent problems in the southern oil-rich regions, with mafia-linked violence – killings and kidnappings. States further north have been afflicted with different kinds of violence, triggered by a complex multiplicity of causes: issues of land ownership, economic deprivation and political control. For example, the nomadic Fulani people who traditionally drive their herds of cattle over these lands have often been associated with tensions arising from competition for scarce resources such as access to water and land for grazing. But for much of the time, these issues have often been settled peaceably.

However, in the last two decades, a religious dimension to intercommunal conflict has become increasingly apparent. Sharia law has been imposed in twelve states. Although, in principle, Shari'a law should not apply to non-Muslims in civil or criminal matters, in reality, Christians have suffered in many ways since its imposition. For example, systematic discrimination against non-Muslims has been reflected in refusal by authorities to grant permission to buy land for building churches or cemeteries. Many churches have subsequently been destroyed as they are deemed to be 'illegal'; Christians applying for jobs or places in higher education frequently experience rejection as soon as it is known that they are not Muslims.

There have been many cases of abduction of Christian girls and their forced marriage to Muslim men. It is claimed that such a 'marriage' is financially rewarded. There have also been cases where Christian girls have been forced to wear Islamic dress in schools and a long-running case where an attempt was made to force Christian nurses working in a state hospital in Bauchi to wear Islamic 'uniforms'. When they refused, claiming that this contravened their religious rights and would confuse their patients, they were dismissed. They appealed – and only after a long saga of court hearings, and an extended period of unemployment, causing severe financial hardship, were they eventually reinstated without having to adopt an Islamic dress code.

Muslims who convert to Christianity are intimidated and receive death threats; they are frequently taken to secure hiding places where they can live safely while receiving instruction and support in their journey of faith as well as preparation for return to the community. The range of discriminatory policies is so comprehensive that, for example, in Kano State, it has led to such a sustained exodus of Christians that the situation has been described as 'attempted religious cleansing'.[1]

The imposition of shari'a law has also been associated

with violence. Over the past two decades, many thousands of Christians have been killed and countless churches, homes and businesses have been destroyed. Traditional believers and Muslims have also suffered. Such violence has also been occurring with increasing frequency in Plateau State, which has not accepted shari'a law but which adjoins states that have done so – Bauchi and Kaduna. Many people now fear that this escalation of violence in Plateau State may be part of a process of Islamization and may reflect a wider agenda by those who would wish to see the process of Islamization spread further afield in Nigeria in ways which might destabilize the nation.

There have been many attacks on Christians in recent years, which have manifest religious motivation. For example, in March 2007, a female schoolteacher in Gombe State reprimanded a student for reading the Koran during a lesson and, when the student was intransigent, she subsequently tried to remove it. Mayhem erupted with allegations of desecration of the holy book. She was savagely assaulted, murdered and her body was burnt. Two days later a church was burnt in the same town. Although sixteen people were arrested for her murder, they were subsequently released and were later heard chanting the names of other Christian teachers.[2]

In March 2009, violence in the capital city of Bauchi State resulted in at least twelve Christians confirmed dead and an unknown number missing, feared dead; fourteen churches were burnt and many homes and businesses belonging to Christians destroyed; 5,000 people were forced to live as refugees in harsh conditions in army barracks. The outbreak of violence was triggered when Christians objected to Muslims using church grounds as a car park. Reports differ as to how the violence began but large mobs of militants shouting Islamic slogans and wearing bandanas attacked and destroyed Christian churches, homes and businesses.

A HART delegation heard many testimonies, including this account by Mercy, aged 19:

> On Saturday morning after breakfast my dad came inside to tell
> us that a COCIN (Christian Church of Nigeria) church was on

fire. Daddy went to the church and I stayed with my younger
brother and sister at home. People knocked down the door
and burst into our home, throwing everything onto the floor.
We were in the kitchen with my 22-year-old uncle. Some of
them were shouting that the house belongs to Muslims and the
Christians should go away. They said they would set the house
on fire. They asked where my mother and father were; I said I
didn't know. They beat my uncle, and cut his head. They said
they would rape my sister and kill us. Then one of them said
they had orders only to kill men. They set my uncle on fire.
I had to watch my uncle burn. When the police came, they
took us out of the house, but they would not rescue my uncle
so I had to listen to his cries for help as he was burnt alive in
the house. The police left him to die. We do not know what
happened to his body.[3]

Christian communities also feel vulnerable as they believe that
the security forces are sometimes complicit with the militants.
In Bauchi, the military reportedly stood by and did not
intervene effectively to protect the Christians. No compen-
sation has been provided by state or federal authorities to assist
the Christian communities in Bauchi with reconstruction of
their destroyed properties.

Also in 2009, in a small town in Bauchi State, a HART
delegation saw the aftermath of the destruction of eight
churches of different denominations, including Anglican,
Roman Catholic, the Evangelical Church of West Africa
[ECWA], Pentecostal and Deeper Life.[4]

In neighbouring Plateau State, the capital city of Jos and
surrounding villages have seen an escalation of violence in
recent years – in 2001, 2004, 2008 and 2010. ECWA is a
well-established organization. The General Secretary gave this
account of developments as they have impacted on ECWA
churches:

We have suffered repeated attacks – in 2001 (when 21 of our
churches were destroyed), in 2004 and again in 2008. On this
occasion we lost 3 of our own churches and a pastorium: it

was a big attack. 22 of our Church leaders have been attacked; one killed. On 28 November at about 1700 the church HQ received a distress call that Muslim youths were attacking, chanting slogans, and breaking into the church premises. Church members were not armed. Security forces tried to reach the victims, but the roads had been blocked by Islamic people. There were 22 people in the church area, which consisted of an auditorium with 5,000 seating capacity, offices and pastorium. Of the 22 trapped in the area, only one person lost his life. They discovered him in an office and broke the wall down. They dragged him out and macheted him; poured petrol over him and burnt him. Then they set the whole building ablaze.[5]

A married lady in Jos with eight children told her story:

I was able to escape the violence because I was warned by a Muslim Yoruba woman, but my home was burnt down. About a hundred of us managed to get on to a pick-up and it took us to safety. 'This trouble has left us nothing! Even my children's clothes are burnt.' All the Christian people who lived in that street have been displaced. Not all escaped. A Wedding Party had come to our neighbourhood. The man and woman had just been married, and were staying in a local house before going the next day to this church for a blessing. They killed the bride and the groom and the relatives who were with them. I will find their names. There were many dead bodies of Christians. They dragged them away. They took them to the mosque.[6]

Fifty thousand Christians were rendered homeless following the 2008 attacks; many continued to live in severe hardship and, when still very vulnerable, Muslims offered to buy the derelict ruins of their homes. Initially, having lost all their possessions, many were tempted to sell, in order to obtain some much-needed resources. However, they subsequently realized that they were victims of a policy designed to expel the Christian communities from key areas in Jos – and that, if they vacated the remains of their homes, they would allow their constituency to change from Christian to Muslim. They therefore decided to resist eviction – and certain districts in Jos are characterized by large numbers of derelict homes with the poignantly defiant sign painted in large letters: THIS HOUSE IS NOT FOR SALE.

In 2010, violence struck again. In March, three villages a few kilometres distance from each other on the outskirts of Jos were simultaneously attacked: Dogonahauwa, Zot and Razat. According to consistent reports by local people, all the attacks occurred at night, starting around 3 a.m. In Dogonahauwa, the attackers came shouting 'Allah Akubar'. They initially fired guns to frighten the villagers and make them run out of their homes. As the villagers fled, many were killed, predominantly with machetes. The attackers then set the village on fire. They were reportedly led by Fulani Muslims settlers who had been living in those areas before relocating to Bauchi. They had lived peacefully alongside the Christians for several years in a Muslim settlement nearby, to the east – and were recognized by their victims. The assailants divided into two groups to attack the village and kill villagers; others followed to burn victims and houses. The local people made repeated phone calls between 3.30 a.m. and 5.30 a.m. pleading for help but as a curfew was in force, no one could travel to them until 6.30 a.m. A police truck arrived about 5.30 a.m. and took some of the wounded to hospital. By the time any help came, the attackers had fled and those who came to help found bodies scattered near their homes, in the market and in fields – and buildings still burning.

Survivors described how the villagers were surrounded and many people were killed as they tried to escape. The main methods of killing were different in the different villages. In Dogonahauwa, people were killed by machete blows on the head and neck. In Zot and Razat, the attackers used guns to shoot their victims. Local people claim that attackers were wearing military uniforms, so they thought these were troops coming to help them – until they realized that they were the attackers. Also, a military unit was stationed nearby, but there was no military intervention to help the villagers under attack. The people claim they have now lost confidence in the military, fearing that some have been complicit in the attacks.

There is still uncertainty about the numbers killed: the military estimate 300; the State Governor, 500; church members counted 450 corpses buried in a mass grave on the day of the attack at Dogonahauwa. The day after the attack, some men were arrested in a Muslim area in Jos East and made statements claiming that they had participated in these attacks as a 'revenge mission' in retaliation for a previous crisis in which some of their own people had been attacked. Although those occurrences had not taken place in this village, they wanted revenge.

Clearly, Muslims have also suffered in the violent clashes – from Christians defending themselves and from security forces, trying to impose control. However, it is difficult to obtain detailed information about the loss of life and property by the Muslim communities, as they do not make information available and as many of their districts have become 'no go' areas for non-Muslims. Officials, even government health workers, are unable to access some of these areas, so it is difficult to ascertain accurate estimates of the situation.

The Christian leaders have consistently tried to prevent retaliation and emphasized the need for forgiveness and reconciliation. However, they are aware that some members of their communities, especially the youth, are strongly inclined to retaliate and that the situation is exacerbated by the lack of confidence among many Christian communities in the impartiality of the security forces. Such lack of confidence is likely to be perpetuated by further attacks, including the killing of over twenty Christians on Christmas Eve, 2010.

Conclusion

Nigeria is a vast nation with such diversity of tribes, cultures and faiths, that it is impossible to make any generalizations about the country as a whole. Even within one state, historical and contemporary issues create complex situations which defy simple interpretations.

However, the evidence shows that the recent attacks in Jos and Bauchi were well prepared and co-ordinated by religiously motivated militants. At a meeting of Christian leaders of all major denominations there was agreement that continuing persecution is to be expected:

> Northern Nigeria will suffer persecution for a long time –
> for the foreseeable future. Christians need a living, vibrant,
> persistent faith to go through what we are going to have to
> go through in the days ahead. Plateau State is being targeted
> because we are an obstacle to the implementation of sharia law.
> Twelve states already have sharia and we resisted it. Therefore,
> we were attacked.

But, despite the attacks, the killings, the injuries, the bereavements and the destruction of churches, homes and livelihoods, the Christian communities are resilient – and growing. When they worship, they worship with such joy, even in the ruins, that they are a living testimony to the fact that God must indeed be 'a very present help in trouble'.

The Anglican Archbishop in Jos, the Most Reverend Benjamin Kwashi and his wife Gloria, have suffered several personal attacks on their family. In 2006, militants came to their home to kill him. He was abroad, so they beat one of his sons and subjected Gloria to horrendous torture. The Archbishop immediately returned home – and within forty-eight hours sent this message of superhuman grace:

> I have now been home for 24 hours and I have had time to sit,
> think, pray – and I had a good laugh. Because I remembered
> how, when I was a little boy, my mother used to pray very hard
> that I would become a Christian. And now, when churches in
> Nigeria get into trouble, Christians in the West pray for us. As it
> is good for Christians in the West to pray, perhaps we should get
> into trouble more often.
>
> I have just come from the hospital where my beloved Gloria

was able to sit to receive Holy Communion – and we praised
God that we had been found worthy to suffer for His kingdom;
and we prayed to God that all Gloria's pain, humiliation and
anguish would be used for His Kingdom, His glory and the
strengthening of His church.

In 2009, he also gave a challenge to the wider Christian
Church:

'If we have a faith worth living for, it is a faith worth dying
for. Do not you [in the West] compromise the faith we are
living and dying for.'

Chapter 13

North Korea: Faithful Unto Death

In August 2010 it was reported that North Korean police had raided a house in Kuwal-dong, in Pyungsung county, Pyongan province, and arrested twenty-three Christians who were worshipping secretly. The three leaders of this underground church were executed, and the remaining twenty believers were sent to a prison labour camp.

A year earlier, on 16 June 2009, another report claimed that a 33-year-old Christian woman, Ri Hyon Ok, was publicly executed for distributing the Bible. In accordance with North Korea's chilling policy of 'guilt by association', three generations of her close family were imprisoned.

Incidents like these, while not uncommon, are not an every day occurrence, not because the authorities show any leniency but because there is so little church activity. North Korea is a country with virtually no religious freedom. Open Doors, Christian Solidarity Worldwide and the US Commission on International Religious Freedom all rank North Korea as the worst persecutor of Christians in the world. Of the approximately 200,000 prisoners of conscience reportedly held in North Korea's brutal labour camps, or gulag, it is believed that between 40,000 and 60,000 are Christians and that they are singled out for some of the worst treatment.

The Kim Dynasty

North Korea's regime is built on a unique philosophy, known as 'Juche' or 'self-reliance'. It is the only current regime in the world which is founded on a dynasty which is treated as a deity. The founding ruler, Kim Il-sung, known as the 'Great

97

leader', is still revered today as a divine being. His embalmed body lies in state in a mausoleum in Pyongyang, his birthday is celebrated as a public holiday, he is worshipped as the 'Eternal President', and when he died in 1994 there was an extraordinary public outpouring of grief.

Kim Il-sung was succeeded upon his death by his son Kim Jong-Il, known as the 'Dear Leader', and all North Koreans are required to keep pictures of father and son in their homes. Severe penalties can be imposed on anyone failing to do so. Even the infamous prison camp at Yodok includes a special shrine to the Great Leader and the Dear Leader, and inmates, despite living in horrific conditions, are required to use a special pair of socks to enter the shrine.

In 2010, the dynasty made preparations to hand power over to a third generation when Kim Jong-Il appointed his youngest son, Kim Jong-Un, aged 27, as a four-star General, a Vice-Chairman of the Central Military Commission and the designated successor.

'Show' churches

The country's constitution states that 'citizens shall have freedom of faith', but this does not reflect the reality. Although there are three officially approved Protestant churches in Pyongyang, a Catholic Cathedral and a Russian Orthodox Church, these are primarily for the benefit of foreign visitors; Korean worshippers are tightly controlled. The Catholic Cathedral has not been permitted to have a priest, making it impossible for the congregation to celebrate Mass. In 1972, a Pyongyang Seminary was allegedly established to train Christian leaders, and in 1988 the Department of Religious Studies was founded at Kim Il-Sung University with courses on Christianity beginning the following year. In 2003, during a parliamentary visit, Caroline Cox attended a service in the Protestant Church at Bongsu in Pyongyang, which was conducted by eighteen Protestant pastors from South Korea, who said they were establishing a Protestant seminary. On a subsequent parliamentary visit in 2010, Caroline Cox and Ben Rogers visited the seminary and met some of the twelve seminarians. They also attended the Sunday morning liturgy at the Russian Orthodox cathedral, celebrated by two North Korean priests who had attended a seminary in Moscow; Russian diplomats attended the service. While these developments can be seen as token gestures to attempt to appease the international community, any opening up of a totalitarian society and any opportunity to introduce a religious faith into an aggressively atheistic society must be welcomed.

Christianity 'public enemy number one'

Outside Pyongyang the harsh reality of North Korea's controlled, oppressive state has been exposed by those who have escaped. One such escapee is Kim Wu-Yeong, who says: 'Christianity is public enemy number one in North Korea.' If someone is a Christian, Kim Wu-Yeong claims, 'they are a political enemy and will either be executed or sent away to a political prison camp'.

Kim personally witnessed the execution of three Christian men, aged 19, 24 and 32, in Musan in June 1998:

> An announcement was made that three men had gone to China and become Christians and were to be executed. People were invited and forced to attend and witness the executions. Each man was blindfolded. They were fully clothed so their injuries could not be completely identified, but none of them could walk on their own. They were dragged out, tied to poles and shot. Normally they would be shot with three bullets, but this time six were used. This was because they had betrayed the regime.

In the 1950s and 1960s, the persecution of Christians in North Korea was especially intense. Kim Il-Sung once said: 'Religion is a reactionary and unscientific view of the world. If they believe in religion, people will see their class

99

consciousness paralyzed and they will no longer be motivated to carry out revolution. Thus we can say that religion is just like opium.'

With that thinking, Kim Il-Sung set about trying to eradicate Christians from North Korea. He associated them with America and the West, and they were killed in the most extraordinarily brutal ways. Some were hung on crosses over fires, crushed by steamrollers or herded off bridges. Such harsh measures successfully eliminated any established church, driving those Christians who had not been killed completely underground.

Such a mentality remains today. A former prison guard, Ahn Myeong-Cheol, says that anti-Christian propaganda continues to be intense:

> Religion is seen to be like opium and has to be wiped out.
> When I was on duty I saw many Christians. One is meant to
> worship only the political leaders and any other worship was a
> deviation from loyalty to the regime. When North Koreans hear
> about God they think they are talking about Kim Il-Sung ... If
> anyone embraces Christianity in North Korea, they are called
> a crazy guy. No one could understand or imagine someone
> wanting to become a Christian.

Other defectors echo these thoughts. One North Korean told the US Commission on International Religious Freedom: 'Religion? Not at all. You cannot say a word about it or three generations of your family can be killed ... Religion was eradicated. We can only serve one person in North Korea, (Kim Jong Il).'

Another said: 'If one says [anything about religion], one immediately gets jailed or killed.'

As defector Soon Ok Lee writes, 'all my life, I had been taught that religion was like a drug ... I was well-trained never to think about God's presence. Having Christians in a nation that believes Kim Il-Sung is a god violates a fundamental belief.' In one of the most extreme examples, she recounts witnessing the horrific murder of eight Christian prisoners. A group of other prisoners were ordered by the guards to pour boiling liquid iron over the Christians. Soon Ok Lee writes in her memoir *Eyes of the Tailless Animals* [AQ]:

> The liquid iron was 1,200 degrees ... They poured the boiling iron on top of the people of God kneeling so quietly. Suddenly, the smell of burning flesh assailed my nostrils. The bodies began to shrivel from the intense heat as the liquid metal burned right through their flesh. I fell to the ground ... In all the years I was in prison, I saw many believers die. Yet they never, never denied the God who is in Heaven. All they had to do was say they don't believe in religion and they would have been released.

North Korea's Christian heritage

The tragedy for North Korea is that prior to the Kim regime, it had a rich Christian heritage and was known as 'the Jerusalem of the East'. Kim Il-Sung himself was raised in a Presbyterian family, his maternal grandfather was a pastor, his father had been educated in missionary schools and he himself was a church organist.

Nevertheless, the Church has a long history of persecution in Korea. Since Christianity first came to the Korean peninsula in the sixteenth century, and developed in the late eighteenth century, it has endured periods of intense persecution. When Queen Chongsun came to the Korean throne in 1800, she unleashed a vicious campaign against Christians, as she considered the faith a heresy harmful to Korean traditions. As Reverend Kim Chang-seok Thaddeus writes in *Lives of 103 Martyr Saints of Korea*: [AQ]

> In 1801, the queen decided to eradicate all Catholics and imprisoned Catholics of all classes. She gave an order to punish the relatives of Catholics. Almost 300 Catholics were killed during this persecution ... After this persecution all Catholics of the nobility were either killed or sent to exile. Those who survived the persecution escaped deep into the mountains, and

many of them starved to death. In these mountainous areas new Catholic communities were formed.

Pope John Paul II described the Church in Korea as 'a community unique in the history of the Church'.

Those words are as accurate a description of North Korea today as they are of the situation 200 years ago – and they apply not only to Catholics but to Christians of all varieties. The testimonies of defectors are consistent: 'I heard the man in the next cell over singing a hymn. He was singing because the security agents had told him to admit he was a Christian and to sing a hymn. He disappeared that night. There were rumours going around that he had been secretly executed.'

Another: 'A woman in her forties ... was found with a Bible in her home and executed in public at a farm threshing floor ... They told me it was because she had kept a Bible. They bound her head, chest and legs and shot her to death in September 2005.'

Eye-witnesses tell of Christians in prison camps trampled to death, or denied food rations and forced to starve.

A flicker of light in the darkness

Despite this seemingly impenetrable darkness, there are occasional flickers of light. In 2003 Caroline Cox and David Alton visited North Korea for the first time. They took with them copies of the Bible, which is illegal in North Korea, and presented them to senior officials in the North Korean regime. Each time, they held the Bible upside down and said simply: 'This is a very important book in our parliamentary tradition. We begin every day's proceedings in the House of Lords and the House of Commons with a reading from this book. We would like to offer you this as a gift, as a sign of respect from one parliamentarian to another'. They left Bibles in the hands of senior North Korean officials, including the President of the Presidium of the Supreme People's Assembly, who is at the top of the hierarchy beneath the 'Dear Leader'. At the end of the meeting with this senior official, he turned to them and spoke these words: 'We know you are Christians. These are very dangerous days for North Korea. Please would you ask Christians in the West to pray for us?

It is said that the establishment of the Russian Orthodox Church in Pyongyang was a direct decision by Kim Jong-il, who was impressed by the churches he saw in Russia. In 2010, he visited a Catholic Church in Jilin, north-eastern China. To penetrate the darkness of North Korea's brutal suppression of religious freedom, perhaps we should be praying that the Kim dynasty might rediscover its own Christian heritage.

Conclusion

In addition we must pray for the secret believers in the world's most closed nation, who risk their very lives for the Lord. May the words of a prayer by an overseas Korean, separated from his homeland, echo in our hearts:

As I look at the skies of home in a foreign land
I too long for the North Korean soil
I pray for that soil of Pyongyang
Though I have never gone, it has been in my prayers all these
    years
That the day may come when those poor North Koreans
Can offer their praise freely
Though my faith be poor, this is my earnest desire
When ... might I set food on that North Korean soil... ?
When ... might I see that day of unification?
The day my grandfather longed to see even in his last
    moments ...?
I pray for them today as well
I do not turn my back on them
I do not forget that my blood is linked with theirs
Lord
Please save them
Please hear their cries.

Chapter 14
Pakistan: A Frontier of Faith

On 2 March 2011 a man described as 'Pakistan's Martin Luther King' and 'the bravest Christian in Pakistan' was gunned down in broad daylight in the capital, Islamabad. Shahbaz Bhatti was Pakistan's Federal Minister for Minorities Affairs, and had defied Islamist extremists by trying to reform the country's notorious blasphemy laws. 'Shahbaz Bhatti died, for all practical purposes, as a martyr – let me be clear – not simply for his Christian faith, but for a vision shared between Pakistani Christians and Muslims,' wrote the Archbishop of Canterbury. 'He was fully aware of the risks he ran. He did not allow himself to be diverted for a moment from his commitment to justice for all.'[1]

Shahbaz was elected to the National Assembly in Pakistan in 2008, and was rapidly promoted to the Cabinet as minister for minorities. His appointment provided religious minorities in Pakistan with a source of hope, for it was the first time an activist of his courage and calibre had been appointed to the post, and the first time the position had been elevated to Cabinet rank. Previous minority representatives have often been token Christians, with little track record of courageous activism. Shahbaz, on the other hand, had been an activist since his school days, and had founded the All Pakistan Minorities Alliance (APMA), bringing Christians and other minorities together in the face of persecution. He told a CSW conference in London in 2009: 'This position [as Minister] cannot change my determination to pursue justice, because I live for religious freedom and I am ready to die for this cause.'

Even before he became a politician, Shahbaz put his life on the line on a daily basis. In 2007, the entire Christian community of Charsadda, a town in Pakistan's Northwest Frontier Province near the border with Afghanistan, had been given ten days to convert to Islam, or face 'dire consequences and bomb explosions'.[2] The threats were made in a letter from the Taliban, circulated among the town's 500-strong Christian population, just days after Pakistan's National Assembly overwhelmingly rejected proposed amendments to the country's notorious blasphemy laws. Similar threats were made to a Bible school in Peshawar and Christians in other parts of the country. On the day of the deadline for the ultimatum, Benedict Rogers telephoned Shahbaz for an update. To his surprise, Shahbaz said he was in Charsadda, to be with the frightened Christians in their hour of need. 'Thank God you have called,' he said. 'I am with the people here, and they are frightened and feel that the world has forgotten them. Now I can tell them that someone outside knows, cares and is praying and speaking for them.'

In the final months of his life, Shahbaz received daily multiple death threats. He recorded a video which he sent to the BBC, to be released in the event of his death. In it he described a profound understanding of Christian faith as his motivation in life. 'I want to share that I believe in Jesus Christ who has given his own life for us,' he said. 'I know what is the meaning of [the] cross. And I am following the cross.'[3]

Attacks on Christians

Harassment and violence are things to which Christians in Pakistan have become increasingly accustomed. In 1997, an entire village of Christians, Shantinagar, 80 km from Bahawalpur, was attacked, and 1,500 homes looted and destroyed.[4] In 2001, four masked gunmen entered a Roman Catholic Church in Bahawalpur as they gathered for worship on a Sunday morning. After killing the security guard at the gate, the gunmen opened fire on the congregation with machine guns. Fifteen worshippers were murdered, including women and children, and a further twenty-five injured. Eyewitnesses claim the gunmen shouted, 'Graveyard of Christians – Pakistan and Afghanistan', adding, 'This is just a start.'[5]

Four years later, militant Islamists in another part of the country called for the elimination of Christians and the public hanging of a Christian accused of blasphemy. A crowd of 3,000 Muslims gathered for Friday prayers at the Jamia mosque in Sangla Hill, 140 miles south of the capital, Islamabad, just weeks after three churches, a school, a convent and Christian homes had been attacked. 'Within minutes, the Christian residential area was blazing. Christian residents fled to save their lives', a report claimed. Muslim clerics used the mosque's loudspeakers to urge Muslims to rise up and eliminate Christians.[6]

In October 2008, a Catholic-run girls' school in Swat, Northwest Frontier Province, was bombed, and was among over 150 girls' schools to be attacked in the course of two years.[7]

In 2009, Pakistan saw some of its worst anti-Christian violence in recent years when a dispute between families in Korian, Punjab, led to a false blasphemy accusation and mob violence against the Christian community in that town and neighbouring Gojra. The violence, which took place between 30 July and 1 August, left eight Christians dead and over a hundred houses destroyed. Six of those killed were burnt alive in their own homes.[8]

In 2010, despite the national outcry in the wake of the Gojra and Korian tragedy, still more Christian communities in Punjab were attacked. On 25 June, twelve gunmen fired bullets into the car of a Christian evangelist, the Reverend Kamran Pervaiz, near Faisalabad.[9] On 1 July, a grenade was thrown in front of St Filian's Church of Pakistan in Sargodha, next to a Christian-owned park where children were playing. On this occasion, it did not explode – but for the children and the church, it was a narrow escape. Four days later in a small village near Sheikhupura, a church building and Christian homes were threatened with demolition by extremists.[10] Frequent reports of individual incidents of anti-Christian violence continue to come out of Pakistan.

Violence against Christian women

Young Christian women and girls are perhaps the most vulnerable in the face of attacks by extremists. Abduction and rape are common. On Easter Day 2007, for example, twelve-year-old Shaheena Masih was kidnapped as she went out to buy her father some juice. The rest of her family were at church, but Shaheena had stayed at home to look after her elderly father, who was unwell. On her way to the shops, four men grabbed her, placing a handkerchief over her mouth. She fell unconscious, but when she woke up, she found herself in a factory. She was gang-raped by the four men, and locked in a room. Shaheena managed to phone her brother from a mobile telephone she found on the floor, but halfway through her conversation, her kidnappers entered the room. They seized the phone, and beat her severely, before taking her to a brothel. 'Don't hesitate to rape a Christian girl,' she had heard them say. 'Even if she dies, no one will get us. Her poor parents cannot pursue us.'[11]

Other victims have been even younger. Seven-year-old Christian girl Sharee Komal was lured away by a Muslim man while playing outside her home in Lahore in 2004. Found hours later near a graveyard under a railway bridge, hysterical, badly bruised and covered in blood, Sharee had been raped and tortured. Five months later, her mother explained what had happened. 'I thought she was dead. The man tried to kill her, by strangling her, and she was badly beaten around the head,' her mother recalled. 'We want justice against this cruelty. It is our opinion that if a Muslim girl is raped, all Muslims come and help. But in our case, because we are Christians, no one has helped.'[12]

Reports from 2010 indicate an increase in incidents of rape targeting Christian women and girls, and emphasize that many rapes are never even registered with the police, particularly where the victim is from a poor family.[13]

In a bitter distortion of justice, some Christian girls who are abducted are forcibly converted to Islam and then their captors are granted custody of them. This happened to Anila and Saba

Masih, kidnapped in southern Punjab in June 2008 while on their way to visit their uncle. They were aged ten and thirteen respectively. Saba was forced to marry one of her kidnappers, and when their father located them and appealed for their return, the Muzaffargarh Sessions Court awarded custody of the two girls to their captors. Only when the case was brought to the Lahore High Court was the ruling overturned – but even then, the two girls were placed in custody in a government-run shelter, and forbidden to see their parents while the case was reconsidered.[14] Two months later, custody of thirteen year-old Saba was awarded to the man who had kidnapped her, while Anila was returned to her parents.[15]

The blasphemy laws

The biggest single cause of religious intolerance, hatred, discrimination and violence in Pakistan is the country's notorious blasphemy laws. Set out in the Pakistan Penal Code, the blasphemy laws are detailed in Section 295. Although based on a law introduced by the British during their colonial rule in India, Pakistan's blasphemy laws were introduced in the 1980s by the then dictator, General Zia ul-Haq. Section 295-C imposes the death penalty on anyone blaspheming the Prophet Mohammed, while Section 295-B carries a life sentence for desecration of the Qu'ran.

Over a thousand people so far have been accused under the blasphemy laws. Those accused are jailed, often tortured and shackled in solitary confinement, and they emerge physically and psychologically scarred. Anyone accused of blasphemy is marked for life in the eyes of the Islamists, so even if they are released from jail and acquitted, neither they nor their family can resume a normal life, and they can instead be forced to live in hiding or exile.

Aslam Masih, for example, suffered serious physical injuries, trauma and memory loss as a result of almost five years in solitary confinement and many severe beatings. An illiterate sheep farmer, he was falsely accused of blasphemy against the Prophet Mohammed and desecration of the Qu'ran by Muslims who did not want a non-Muslim farming business to succeed in the local area. He was given two life sentences and a fine of 100,000 rupees (1,300 pounds sterling) on 7 May 2002, and 100 mullahs stood outside the court during his trial. He was acquitted upon appeal but lives in hiding. 'He has no choice but to live in hiding. He lives in danger,' his lawyer said. 'A normal life is not possible for a former blasphemy prisoner in this society, even if he has been acquitted.'[16]

Since 1986 several people have been sentenced to death, though subsequently acquitted. The death sentence was handed out to a woman for the first time in November 2010, in the case of Asia Bibi (a Christian), sparking an international outcry. While no one has yet been executed by the state, at least thirty-three people have been arbitrarily killed by vigilante extremists in circumstances triggered by blasphemy accusations, eight of those in the Gojra and Korian attacks, mentioned above. On 19 July 2010 two Christians accused of blasphemy were shot dead outside a courthouse. The Reverend Rashid Emmanuel and his brother Sajid Emmanuel were killed days after handwriting experts had informed the police that the signatures on papers insulting the Prophet Mohammed did not match those of the accused. They were expected to be acquitted, but instead were gunned down in broad daylight as they were being led back to jail. The previous week, hundreds of Muslims marched to the predominantly Christian area of Dawood Nagar, calling for the immediate death of the two Christians and chanting 'hang the blasphemers'. The mob reportedly shouted obscenities about Christ, Christians and Christianity, and attacked a local Catholic Church. Three days before the murder of the two Christians, loudspeakers from a mosque in Waris Pura blared announcements urging Muslims to 'burn the houses of Christians'.[17]

It is not only the accused whose lives are endangered. Lawyers and human rights activists who defend blasphemy cases or campaign for the law's repeal are at risk. In blasphemy cases, extremists – usually led by mullahs – crowd into the courtroom, shouting blood-curdling threats to the judge and defence counsel.

While many Christians have been affected by the blasphemy laws and non-Muslims are more susceptible to extra-judicial killing after an accusation, every Pakistani is vulnerable, regardless of religion. When the laws were first introduced, they were used primarily as a tool by extremists to target religious minorities, but then Muslims began to use the law against each other to settle personal scores. The law is so open to abuse, because it requires no evidence other than an accusation made by one person against another. There is no question of intent, and an inadequate definition of blasphemy. When it comes to court the accuser does not even always have to substantiate the charge. In some cases, when the judge has asked what the accused actually said, the accuser has refused to elaborate, on the basis that by repeating the alleged statement they themselves would be blaspheming.

The impact of the blasphemy laws was highlighted very dramatically in 1998, when one of Pakistan's leading campaigners for justice, the Catholic Bishop of Faisalabad, Bishop John Joseph, stood in front of the court building in Sahiwal and shot himself dead. In what was a pre-planned protest following the death sentence imposed on Ayub Masih, a Christian accused of blasphemy, Bishop John Joseph made the ultimate sacrifice in the hope that it would underscore the need for the repeal of these unjust laws. A few days previously, he had told friends that if the blasphemy laws were not repealed, 'we will launch a protest which will stun the whole world'. In a letter to the Vatican, sent following seven days of prayer and fasting, the Bishop wrote: 'I only hope and pray that God accepts the sacrifice of my blood for his people.'[18]

Hope

Did Bishop John Joseph, and thirteen years later Shahbaz Bhatti, die in vain? It is easy to believe that they did, because the situation has certainly worsened dramatically in recent years. In the months following Asia Bibi's sentencing at the end of 2010, the blasphemy debate became dangerously volatile, leading to the assassination of Salmaan Taseer, the then Governor of Punjab, and Shahbaz Bhatti. The government, which had previously shown signs that it might support reform, denied any intention to amend the blasphemy laws – a significant u-turn and a major setback.

Yet the Christians maintain extraordinary faith despite the pressure they face, and there are a number of inspiring Christian activists who, with great courage and determination, continue the struggle for religious freedom and justice. Lawyers who defend those accused of blasphemy, often facing death threats and assassination attempts themselves, hold a flame of hope. Leading activists such as former Pakistani fighter pilot and war veteran Group Captain (Rtd) Cecil Chaudhry, and APMA, refuse to buckle under the pressure of intimidation. Cecil Chaudhry led the campaign for the restoration of the joint electorate system, bringing to an end the religious apartheid that had existed in which Christians could only vote for Christian candidates in elections and Muslims could only vote for Muslims. The separate electorate system was, second only to the blasphemy laws, one of the most significant contributing factors to religious segregation, hostility and violence, and it made non-Muslims second-class citizens. Achieving its abolition was a major victory, and a source of hope for Christians and other minorities. A few days after the assassination of Shahbaz Bhatti, Cecil Chaudhry vowed to continue the struggle. 'We're ready to lay down our lives. We will continue his commitment for a repeal of the blasphemy laws. How many of us will they kill? It doesn't make any difference,' he told the Sunday Times.[19]

Conclusion

On Saturday 11 August 2007 thousands of Christians, other religious minorities and moderate Muslims gathered at Minar-e-Pakistan, the 'National Monument' in Iqbal Park,

Lahore, three days before the country celebrated the sixtieth anniversary of its creation. The rally was held on the site where the Lahore Declaration was passed in 1940 calling for the creation of a separate state of Pakistan. Those assembled in 2007 unanimously endorsed a 'Charter of Demands', calling on the government of Pakistan to ensure equal rights for religious minorities, and the repeal of the blasphemy laws that, it says, cause minorities to live in 'perpetual fear'. The national rally was organized by APMA.

Pakistan today is very different from the country its founder, Mohammed Ali Jinnah, envisaged, but Jinnah's vision is the one to embrace if Christians and other minorities are to have a chance of peace. In 1947, Jinnah said these famous words:

> You are free. You are free to go to your temples. You are free to go to your mosques or to any other places of worship in this state of Pakistan. You may belong to any religion, caste or creed – that has nothing to do with the business of the state ... We are starting with this fundamental principle, that we are all citizens and citizens of one state.

However impossible the task may seem, may the God of the impossible make that vision a reality.

Chapter 15

Sri Lanka: A Crossroad of Faiths

In the rubble of the burnt-out church in Kesbewa, just outside Colombo, a group of ladies gathered the children around them for the beginning of Sunday school. Amid the children's chatter, the ladies had an extraordinary calm as they prepared to teach Bible stories about Moses, Jonah, Daniel and, of course, Jesus. A graceful silence descended as the children were brought to order and the class began. If the charred remains, the broken stones and the open sky had not spoken of the attack this church had endured, it would have appeared like any other Sunday school.[1]

Eighteen months previously, on 24 September 2003 a mob attacked the Assemblies of God Church at Kesbewa at 1 p.m. in the morning. The church was completely burned down. It was not the first time the church had been attacked, but it was the most severe attack. Earlier that year, the church was subjected to many incidents when mobs threw stones, rocks and burning oil at the church. On one occasion, masked men on motorbikes threw homemade bombs at the church, injuring an eighteen- year-old boy on his arm and back.

Pastor Kumara, who established the church in 1984, was attacked several times. On one occasion he was punched in the face by a man with rings on his fingers, causing him to lose a front tooth as a result. His home was circled by people at night several times, and he had been followed in his car. Hate literature had been distributed locally, and posters displayed on billboards in the village. One proclaimed: 'Buddhists and Sinhalese to stand up and protect Buddhism for future generations'; another announced 'Let's beat the conspiracy to destroy Buddhism in Sri Lanka'; yet another called all Buddhists to a special meeting in the temple to discuss 'the people's protection'. It was not long after this meeting that the church was burned down.[2]

Violence against Christians

Violence against Christians in Sri Lanka is a little known feature of the island's troubled history. Sri Lanka is well known for its wider civil war between the government and the Liberation Tigers of Tamil Eelam (LTTE), which came to an end in 2009 after twenty-five years. The conflict was primarily ethnic rather than religious, separate from the growing hostility towards Christians generated by increasingly militant Buddhists, although there was some overlap. The Sinhalese majority is Buddhist, while the Tamils are predominantly Hindu, but Christianity is the only religion found among both Sinhalese and Tamils. The Church was sometimes seen to have assisted the Tamils, and for extreme Sinhalese Buddhists religion is integral to nationalism and identity – in their eyes, to be Sinhalese is to be Theravada Buddhist.[3] Yet besides Sinhalese Buddhist nationalism, the main factors behind the increase in violence and hostility against Christians were separate, and more to do with the growth of the Church, the activities of evangelicals and the legacy of colonialism.

Attacks on churches and individual Christians have come in waves in Sri Lanka in recent years. From 2003–2004, the National Christian Evangelical Alliance of Sri Lanka (NCEASL) recorded over 150 acts of violence against churches and Christian communities, and claimed that at least 140 churches were forced to close due to attack, intimidation and threats. On Christmas Eve 2003, twenty churches were attacked in one night, and many churches celebrated Christmas with police and army protection. In February 2004 a mob wrote the words 'the Church is finished' on the wall of the Apostolic Church in Boraluwewa.[4]

All this was a significant increase from previous years, and would be followed by a similar lull in subsequent years. In 2000, only fourteen incidents were reported, and only thirteen in 2001 and 2002. From 2005 until 2008, although regular incidents continued to occur, the violence subsided from the levels of 2003-2004, but in 2006 it escalated again for a brief period, and in 2008 violence flared up once more.

In February 2006, the pastor of a Dutch Reformed Church in Galle was warned that if he visited neighbouring Hikkaduwa, his limbs would be 'torn off' and he would be killed.[5] In August 2006, a mob of 200, accompanied by three Buddhist monks, attacked a Christian-run children's home, and planted a Buddhist flag on the roof. They assaulted the staff and threatened to kill the couple in charge. The staff were warned if they did not leave, they would be 'burned alive'.[6]

On 3 March 2008 the Zion Mount Prayer House in Mulaitvu District was set on fire. The pastor, his wife, child and two others were believed to have been inside at the time, although they escaped. The previous day, ten Bible school students in Lunuwila, Putlam District, were attacked by ten masked men on motorbikes, and were beaten, kicked and assaulted with rods. The same day, a mob of 200 threatened to kill a pastor in Udugama, Galle District, if he did not leave the village.[7] In June that year, four anti-Christian rallies were held in Hambanthota District, and a Christian girl was attacked by her fellow students.[8]

Since 2009 violence against Christians has declined significantly, however the militant Buddhists have employed other tactics.

Anti-conversion legislation

The most serious threat to religious freedom in Sri Lanka has come in the form of proposed anti-conversion legislation. The proposal has been discussed in various guises since 2002, when it was first made by the Minister of Hindu Cultural Affairs after he had visited the Indian state of Tamil Nadu. Tamil Nadu was one of five states in India which at the time had anti-conversion laws, although its legislation was repealed in 2006. The government in Sri Lanka took up the minister's proposal, and drafted a 'Freedom of Religion Bill' which appeared to ban conversions altogether. Since 2004, however, the government has not attempted to introduce the bill in Parliament, and as far as it is concerned the idea appears to have been shelved.[9]

Pressure for anti-conversion laws has continued, however, from militant Buddhists. In 2003, a new political party consisting of Buddhist monks was formed. The Jathika Hela Urumaya (JHU) won nine seats in Parliament in 2004, and in 2007 became a coalition partner in President Mahinda Rajapaksa's government. After the death of a high-profile Buddhist monk, the Venerable Gangodawila Soma Thero, in 2003, the JHU launched a major campaign for the introduction of an anti-conversion law. The idea was a key election campaign pledge, and led to the introduction of a private member's bill in 2004. The Supreme Court, however, ruled on 10 August 2004 that parts of the proposed legislation were unconstitutional, and the JHU agreed to amend it. Since then, the bill has not been tabled in Parliament, but there are continuing fears that the proposal remains on the agenda.

The very existence of an anti-conversion law would severely undermine freedom of religion and belief in Sri Lanka. Even if such legislation was never used and no one was ever convicted, it would lend legitimacy to threats and intimidation of religious minorities, worsen religious tensions, and engender violence and persecution. The draft legislation as it currently stands contains serious flaws, including poor definitions of the 'crimes' it seeks to prohibit and grossly disproportionate penalties. For example, advocates of the proposed legislation claim they are not seeking to ban all conversions, simply forcible conversions and allurement. Yet their definitions of forced conversion and allurement are extraordinarily vague. 'Allurement', for example, is defined in the draft bill as 'the offer of any temptation' in the form of 'a gift or gratification', 'a grant of any material benefit' or 'the grant of employment'. Christian charitable activity or educational services could clearly be construed as illegitimate under this bill. 'Force' is defined as 'a show of force' including 'a threat of harm or injury or any kind of religious disgrace or condemnation'. Anyone convicted under this law would face a five-year jail term and a fine of 150,000 rupees (£800), which is higher than the penalty for rioting armed with a lethal weapon.

'Unethical conversions'?

There are two major factors behind this proposed legislation. First, militant Buddhists are angered by the growth of the Church. In part, this is due to their militant Sinhalese Buddhist nationalism, but it cannot be denied that the behaviour of some over-enthusiastic evangelicals has contributed to the situation. Nothing whatsoever justifies the violence against Christians or the introduction of anti-conversion laws, but Christians must examine themselves and take responsibility for contributing to religious tensions. While most Christians share their faith responsibly, acting in a culturally-sensitive and respectful way towards their Buddhist neighbours, Buddhists complain about some over-zealous activities. Loud and exuberant praise and worship services and charismatic all-night prayer sessions can be disturbing for Buddhist neighbours, for example. Christian forms of worship, both traditional and Pentecostal, are seen as 'Western' and, in the words of one pastor, 'not rooted in local soil'.[10] Pastors wear suits and the songs and instruments are Western. If the Sri Lankan Church developed its own worship songs, using traditional instruments, they might help overcome this perception that they belong to a 'foreign' religion.

Some Christian evangelists have been disrespectful of Buddhism, and there are suggestions that in some areas, converts to Christianity have been ordered to smash and destroy their Buddhist statues and symbols. Understandably, these actions are not conducive to religious harmony. As Reverend Noel Fernando has said:

> We Christians do have a mandate to share the Gospel, but God has also given us a head to think about whether we will offend people ... Understanding cross-cultural ministry is very important. We need to build a bridge of friendship with others, but some Christians simply barge in and want to force their faith upon others.[11]

However, it is equally important to recognize that the majority of Christians have tried to meet the militant Buddhists

117

halfway, and many of the allegations are grossly exaggerated or completely fabricated. Several Christian groups, including the NCEASL, have drawn up codes of conduct for evangelism and for humanitarian activities, and have offered alternative ways of addressing the concerns of Buddhists. The three major church organizations – the Catholic Bishops Conference, the National Christian Council and NCEASL – have proposed establishing a mechanism for tackling grievances and allegations of insensitive or illegitimate behaviour, through inter-faith dialogue. A 'Religious Harmony Commission' has been suggested, to include five eminent people not active in any religious group, to arbitrate disputes, and NCEASL has proposed that an equal number of representatives of different religions work together to investigate grievances. These ideas have met with silence from the militant Buddhists.

While they admit that Christians have made mistakes and behaved insensitively on occasions, the churches refute talk of 'unethical' conversions. The term is used in particular in reference to the Church's involvement in aid and social action, but Christian leaders from all major denominations in Sri Lanka deny that such humanitarian work is ever conditional on conversion. Unproven allegations have been made that foreign missionaries are paid based on the number of converts they make, and that converts themselves are paid money to change their religion. Such claims are inflammatory and, thus far, without foundation.

Hate propaganda

Some claims, however, are even wilder and are purely absurd. The death of the Buddhist monk, the Venerable Gangodawila Soma Thero, in 2003 was blamed on Christians, even though he died of old age in hospital. Newspapers published provocative articles. *Lankadeepa* ran a story headlined 'Soma Thero did not die; he was killed', while *Dhivayina* claimed that the monk was admitted to hospital by a Christian pastor and therefore his death was 'a conspiracy'.

In some of the most extreme allegations, which would be comical if the consequences were not so serious, Christians have been accused of making cookies with the image of Buddha on them and producing underwear with Buddha's image, in a deliberate attempt to insult Buddhism. It is hard to imagine any Christians being involved in any such activity. The destruction of Buddhist images in Afghanistan by the Taliban was even blamed on Christians – the idea of Christians in league with the Taliban is certainly beyond credibility.

Christian aid agencies have been the target of false propaganda too, with *The Buddhist Times* running headlines such as 'Conversions under false premises: World Vision', with sub-heads in one story about World Vision suggesting 'Buddhist and Muslim children on the Christian auction block?' and 'Kidnapping children for God?' Another headline read: 'Buddhism and Hinduism under assault'.

In addition to the newspaper headlines, leaflets and billboards shriek furious headlines. Pamphlets with titles such as 'Converting Buddhists to Christianity is a money-making racket,' 'Defeat the Christian invasion and defend the Buddha Sasana,' and 'Buddhists wake up! Protect Buddhism from the Christian invaders' are distributed widely.[12]

Killings

Compared with some countries, the Sri Lankan Church has suffered mercifully few martyrs. There have, however, been a few prominent cases. As early as 1988, before the campaign against Christians became concerted, Pastor Lionel Jayasinghe was murdered. He had been a Buddhist monk, and had converted to Christianity in 1980 at the age of twenty-two. He married his wife, Lalani, in 1986 and they founded a church together. Local Buddhists were opposed to the presence of the church, and tensions grew. On the night of 25 March 1988, two men came to the house to meet Pastor Lionel. Within a few minutes, Lalani heard a gunshot, and her husband stumbled into the bedroom, having been shot in the face. The attackers pursued him, stabbed him and shot him again – in front of Lalani.

Ten years later, on 17 February 2008, another pastor was murdered. Pastor Neil Edirisinghe was shot dead, and his wife was shot and wounded.[13]

The faith, courage, intellect and hard work of the Christian leaders in Sri Lanka, however, gives cause for hope. In 2004, after the JHU had tabled their draft anti-conversion bill, critics were given seven days to launch a legal challenge on constitutional grounds. Over twenty organizations joined forces, including the NCEASL, the NCC and the Catholic Bishop of Chilaw, to petition the Supreme Court. Their efforts paid off, and the JHU was forced by the Supreme Court to amend the bill, and the legislation has not been taken forward.[14] Christian advocates have shown a remarkable ability to document incidents and bring the issues to the attention of the international community, which has shown more interest and with greater impact than perhaps expected. An Early Day Motion in 2004 in the British House of Commons, signed by over 150 Members of Parliament, condemning attacks on Christians, was drawn to the attention of the Sri Lankan President and Cabinet by the Foreign Minister, just when the government was discussing anti-conversion legislation. It is believed that such international attention helped convince the government to put the idea on hold.

With violence having significantly declined and anti-conversion legislation apparently on the backburner, the situation for Christians in Sri Lanka may appear to have improved, although the predicament of many Tamil Christians and Hindus remains dire.

There are serious and perhaps more insidious challenges for the Church which mean that our persecuted brothers and sisters continue to require our prayers. The government has co-opted Sinhala Buddhist nationalist rhetoric, resulting in the exclusion of religious minorities and Tamils, and it shows little interest in national reconciliation. There is talk of the introduction of a 'protection of Buddhism' bill, which might go further than anti-conversion legislation. Non-governmental organizations are facing increasing restrictions, and this particularly affects Christian groups. Human rights defenders, including those motivated by their Christian faith, are facing severe harassment. In this context, Christians still have more work to do to develop a culturally sensitive and appropriate biblical faith, while staying strong in the face of opposition.

Conclusion

Despite the persecution of Christians, and the wider human rights violations associated with the civil war, there is hope for the beautiful island of Sri Lanka. For example, people like Lalani are living testimonies to the power of reconciliation. She has continued to run the church she founded with her husband, even after his murder. Over the years, she has received threats and her house has been stoned. Bombs were placed in the church, and on several occasions her property was burned down. Yet she has persisted with her ministry and, as a result, has won the respect of her previously hostile neighbours.

Chapter 16

Sudan: Smiling Through the Pain

In 1995, in the midst of a desolate, barren landscape in southern Sudan, with every kind of human habitation burnt to the ground, a bedraggled group of emaciated people gather excitedly under a tree to attend Mass. Bishop Macram Gassis, the exiled Roman Catholic Bishop of El Obeid has just flown in with Caroline Cox, illegally, to bring help and encouragement to his people suffering in a war being waged against them by the National Islamic Front regime, based in Khartoum, which seized power by military coup in 1989.

Underneath the sheltering branches of the tamarind tree, the Bishop looked with profound compassion on his flock – decimated by starvation, enslavement and bombardment – and made this poignant address:

> Here we are, in this beautiful cathedral, not made by human hands, but by nature and by God – and it is filled with the people of God, and especially with children. You people here in Sudan still smile, in spite of suffering, persecution and slavery. Your smiles put us to shame. Many of you have been captured and taken into slavery. If that happens to you or to those whom you love, remember that that is not real slavery. The real slave is a person who does injustice to brothers and sisters and who kills them. But you are children of God … no longer slaves, but free: children of liberty and truth.
>
> Many of you are naked and embarrassed by your nakedness. Don't be embarrassed. Yours is not true nakedness. True nakedness is to be without love. Therefore, be clothed in love – that is true Christianity – and show your love to those who do not know our Lord of love.
>
> Do not think that we will forget you. You will be

remembered as those who are closest to God, because every day you are obeying Christ's command to take up His cross and to follow Him.

We will pray for you – but prayer without deeds is dead, as love without action is dead. Our prayer and our love must be in action for you.

I came, I saw, I heard, I touched – and I am enriched.

Since attaining independence from Britain in 1956, Sudan, Africa's largest nation – a land the size of Europe but with an estimated population of only about 50 million – has been afflicted by many years of civil war. The nation is split between a predominantly Arab, Islamic north and an African south with a majority of Christians or traditional believers. There are also the so-called 'marginalized areas': the Nuba Mountains (southern Kordofan), Abyie and southern Blue Nile. The peoples of these regions are predominantly African with mixed religious affiliations – Muslims, Christians and traditional believers – who traditionally have lived peaceably with each other in their own communities.

Inter-communal conflicts associated with competition for scarce resources such as land, water and cattle, have been historically commonplace. But the scale and intensity of violence escalated dramatically in the early 1980s when the Islamic government in Khartoum attempted to introduce shari'a law to Bor, one of the southern cities. This was fiercely resisted and a senior army officer, John Garang, was dispatched to subdue the conflict. Instead, he joined the rebels and became the leader of the Sudan People's Liberation Army (SPLA) and its civilian movement the Sudan People's Liberation Movement (SPLM).

In 1989, an Islamist regime – the National Islamic Front – took power by military coup and quickly declared military Jihad (Islamic holy war) against all who opposed it. The objectives were twofold: the Islamization of non-Muslims and the Arabization of the African peoples. The methods included military offensives against civilians, the manipulation of aid and slavery.[1]

This war lasted until a Comprehensive Peace Agreement (CPA) was signed in 2005 – but only after two million had died, four million had been displaced and tens of thousands of people, predominantly women and children, had been abducted and taken into slavery. The conflict then moved to Darfur, where the victims were predominantly Muslim Africans.

The legacy of the war against the peoples of southern Sudan and the marginalized areas is a scenario of devastation: a 'lost generation' of children who could not go to school because of constant aerial bombardment and some of the worst health statistics in the world. One in seven mothers in southern Sudan die in pregnancy or childbirth; one in seven children die before the age of five years; and only 17 per cent of the population receive immunization, leaving 83 per cent vulnerable to potentially killer diseases such as diphtheria, tuberculosis, tetanus, measles and whooping cough.

There are deep concerns among the Christian communities of the South that Islam is using the humanitarian crisis to promote conversions to Islam. During the war, many Christians preferred to die from hunger or disease rather than accept aid from government of Sudan sources, which required conversion to Islam as a precondition of aid. This agonizing choice was epitomized by a young, virtually naked blind mother in 1994 in Bahr-El-Ghazal, holding her child who was dying of starvation, who said, with anguish: 'I could go to another area where the government of Sudan is in charge and receive food, medicine, clothes. But I know that if I do, I will have to convert to Islam – and that I will not do. We are Christians – and I would prefer to live and die as Christians.' While this would be a challenging decision to make for oneself, it must be infinitely, unimaginably harder to make the decision to sacrifice one's child. Such is the price paid by countless people in Sudan who refused survival for themselves and their children in order not to betray their faith.

With humanitarian crises taking place in many parts of Sudan there is now a fear that this kind of conditional Islamic aid is being used in order to promote Islamization. Christian leaders in southern Sudan have a document with a budget for 'Proposal for the Islamization of southern Sudan'. This identifies costs for teacher training, schools, school textbooks, hospitals, staff salaries, medication, uniforms – with a total budget of U$29 million. It is believed this has been sent to Saudi Arabia and Libya and that the money is pouring in to provide aid as a means of conversion to Islam. Anglican, Presbyterian and Roman Catholic bishops in the South have expressed concern: 'We are losing in peace our religious freedom which we managed to hold on to at such terrible cost in the war.'

In May, 2007, the Roman Catholic Bishop Daniel Adwok Kur of Khartoum claimed that the Khartoum government was using the Darfur crisis as 'a smokescreen to spread Islam into the mainly Christian south'. Giving a keynote address to an Aid to the Church in Need conference in Scotland, he said that Khartoum is working with Islamic organizations in the Middle East to fund mosques, schools and hospitals with the specific aim of evangelization: 'The government is ringing the same bell of Islamizing Sudan while at the same time talking about the importance of the CPA.'[2]

While the CPA is designed to give the people of southern Sudan the opportunity to decide whether to remain part of a 'United Sudan' or to opt for Independence, those living in the marginalized areas have no such choice. The CPA merely offered a vague 'consultation' with no option to secede from control by Khartoum.

At the time of writing, it is widely expected that the vast majority in January 2011, 98% of the peoples of the South voted for secession. The Roman Catholic Archbishop of Juba explained why this would probably be the case: he stressed the peoples of the South have suffered for far too long in a 'United Sudan' from Arab oppression and attempted Islamisation. He believed that the North would wish to maintain a 'United Sudan' for reasons of political power and wealth, especially associated with oil, while Southerners would vote for Independence to preserve their African identity and religious freedom.

As it is widely known that the North does not want secession to occur, there is fear that measures may be taken to reignite conflict – directly, or through Khartoum's use of surrogates such as armed local militias or the notorious Lord's Resistance Army [LRA] which caused suffering on a massive scale in northern Uganda and is still perpetrating atrocities in the Democratic Republic of the Congo and southern Sudan.

There is also concern for the peoples in the marginalized areas who are deeply unhappy with their plight. When Khartoum tried to impose shari'a law in Kadugli (in the Nuba mountains – or southern Kordofan, as the region has been renamed since the CPA, against the wishes of local people), this was fiercely resisted by the local people – both Muslim and Christian – and seen as a portent of Khartoum's intentions to impose its hardline version of Islam. As the Nuba Mountain people have a famously rich local culture, including their distinctive dancing, music and wrestling, they are intensely dismayed at the prospect of losing it to an ideologically incompatible regime. Moreover, since administrative control of their region was transferred to Khartoum under the CPA, the Nuba Mountain people have been denied access to resources from countries to the South, especially Kenya and Uganda, being forced to rely, instead, on Khartoum. They claim that Khartoum has been ruthlessly manipulative, denying aid and resources to non-Muslim organizations to such an extent that, to quote a local leader: 'We are even worse off now, under the CPA, than we were during the war.' And the people feel so desperate that, when southern Sudan becomes independent, they may feel that they have no option but to return to war.

While the situation in the South and the marginalized areas is cause for great concern, the plight of the people in the North is also deeply disturbing. Here, citizens are subject to shari'a law, as interpreted by the National Congress Party – the Islamist successor to the NIF regime. The strict ban on apostasy, with conversion from Islam carrying the risk of execution by public authorities or family members, means that Christian religious organizations cannot use names with Christian connotations and they, as well as the churches, are severely limited in their activities. Secular organizations and journalists have also been subject to repressive measures, with sporadic fierce clamp-downs and punitive measures taken against those who criticize the ruling elites.

Another cause for concern is the suffering endured by tens of thousands of southerners who fled to the North during the war and have since been consigned to lives of extreme impoverishment and deprivation in huge camps for internally displaced peoples (IDPs) around Khartoum. They are immensely vulnerable and their future plight is very uncertain, especially now the South has voted for independence.

The causes for concern in northern Sudan are legion – to the extent that the Northern Bishops of the Episcopal Church of the Sudan issued a statement on 22 July 2010:

On the current situation in Sudan

We, the Bishops from Northern Sudan of the Episcopal Church (Anglican) representing the Dioceses of Khartoum, El Obeid, Kadugli, Wad Medani, Port Sudan and Kassala Area, met to reflect, review, meditate and to pray for the current political situation in our beloved Country.

'This is a historic period in the history of Sudan. After the referendum in 2011 Sudan will never be the same again, whether it remains united or becomes two countries. Time is short and urgent reflection and actions are needed to ensure a peaceful future. This is Sudan's Kairos Moment. It is time to choose life. We have no time to waste.'

The Church in North Sudan:

Life has always been difficult for Christians and other marginalized people living in the North. We have great concern about the future of the Church in the North in the advent of the referenda. We therefore call upon all the stakeholders to put in place appropriate measures to protect Christians and the marginalized people in the North. We also call upon the governments of Sudan and South Sudan and the International Community to assist the IDPs to return to their original places voluntarily; and to safeguard the rights of the Christians in the North, most especially if the results of the referenda opt for secession.

We call upon our faithful to commit themselves into prayer and fasting in these coming days, for a peaceful transition and that people will not go back to war again and that all will accept the results of referenda and popular consultations.

The Rt Revd Yousif Abdalla Kuku, Bishop of Port Sudan

The Rt Revd Andudu Adam Elnail, Bishop of Kadugli

The Rt Revd Samaan Farjalla, Bishop of Wad Medani

The Rt Revd Ismail Gebriel Abudigi, Bishop of El Obeid

The Rt Revd Ezekiel Kondo, Bishop of Khartoum

The Rt Revd Abdu Elnur Kodi, Assistant Bishop of Port Sudan, Kassala

Conclusion

Despite, and through, all the suffering endured by the Christian churches in Sudan, faith survives and grows; the people worship with joy and the indomitable Sudanese smile lights up the faces of people, however dark their predicament. We finish with two emblematic examples of this witness of light and joy even in the midst of the darkest days of the war.

Caroline Cox met a Roman Catholic catechist, Santino Ring on a visit to Mayen Abun, in Bahr-el-Ghazal in May, 1998. He had been away from the little town on a pastoral visit, when many hundreds of government of Sudan forces, supported by Mujahidin (Islamic Jihad warriors) and Murahaleen (local tribesmen recruited and resourced by government forces) swept through the area, killing humans and cattle, burning homes and crops and abducting women and children into slavery. He returned to find his sister and her husband had been killed and many other villagers slaughtered – some tied up and thrown into a burning hut and others with their throats cut. Homes and crops had been destroyed – and he only had tamarind seeds with which to try to feed his sister's four children. Desperate, he pleaded:

Sudan: Smiling Through the Pain

We here in southern Sudan are trying to hold a frontline of Christianity for the rest of the world, against a regime that wants to spread Islam throughout Sudan and the rest of Africa. The regime in Khartoum is spending a million dollars a day on this war. And we have nothing. And we are all alone. You are the first Christians even to visit us…

And then the ultimately poignant challenging plea:

Doesn't the Church want us any more?

Despite the agony, the loneliness and the sense of being entirely forgotten, the next morning Santino led service in the remains of the church – a service that was full of grace, joy and gratitude. The bedraggled congregation sat mostly on the hard floor, among the remains of burnt Bibles and slashed drums. Old and young were perilously emaciated; many were virtually naked; some were coughing with chest infections, possibly tuberculosis. A few of the most elderly were sitting on some makeshift wooden benches which served as pews. As a catechist, Santino could not celebrate Mass, but he followed the liturgy as far as was appropriate and he preached. As he spoke, his face was transformed with love and joy – and he urged his flock to rejoice in all God's goodness and gifts, saying, with no hint of irony: 'See how much we have to be thankful for – we even have some seats to sit on.'

Far away, to the eastern side of southern Sudan, similar joy was manifest in Gumriak, in Western Upper Nile. As Caroline Cox and her colleagues came in to land at a small airstrip, they could see smoke from burning villages from horizon to horizon. As they landed, emaciated people came running up to welcome then, saying they were so glad to see the visitors, because they thought the world had forgotten them. They then described how they had been the targets of an attack by government of Sudan forces a few days previously. Aerial bombardment had preceded ground offensives and the large craters were clearly visible. As a result of the attacks, 6,000 homes had been destroyed as well as ten churches, seven mosques and many other buildings. The visitors, walking through the blackened remains of the ruins of this scorched earth policy, were feeling as black as the surroundings, when suddenly they were surprised by singing and the sounds of celebration: into the midst of this scenario of destruction came a joyful catechist. He had just returned from spending several weeks walking through the bush to remote villages, taking the Good News of the Gospel. He had baptized 7,000 Christians and established eleven new churches.

Here, as in so many places and at so many times throughout the history of the Church, the Church flourishes in the fires of persecution. The buildings may be destroyed but the Church not only survives – it grows – and there is much to celebrate in and through the suffering. The famous Sudanese smiles remain, invincible, to the glory of God.

Chapter 17

Vietnam: Beaten Not Broken

The Hmong Christians in Cu Hat village, Dak Lak province, were proud of their new church building. They had scraped together all the resources they had and by September 2008, they had enough materials to construct a 12 × 20 metre wooden church building, large enough to provide a space for 500 Christians to worship. They had also managed to give the building a tile roof that would last through the rainy season. They celebrated and praised God.

The mood of celebration did not last long, however. Within weeks, local authorities told them that they had constructed the church illegally, and ordered them to tear it down. They were told if they did not destroy their church 'voluntarily', the authorities would do it themselves. On 18 December 2008 that threat turned into a reality.

At 7 a.m., literally hundreds of government officials, police and demolition workers arrived at the church, and within an hour and a half the beautiful church building, which the Hmong Christians had sacrificed so much to build, was in ruins. The authorities took the good quality wood away for their own use, and police kept those Christians who tried to intervene at bay with electric cattle prods. Five Christians were seriously injured, including a pregnant woman who was poked in the back with an electric cattle prod. Police stepped on a four-year-old child, breaking his arm.

Some signs of hope?

Such brutal treatment of Christians is not uncommon in Vietnam, although it appears in recent years to have occurred in localized areas and is not as widespread throughout the entire country as it used to be. More churches report being able to worship without harassment or interference. A 2006 training manual for government officials in the Northwest Highlands, issued by the Committee on Religious Affairs, included a plan to 'resolutely subdue the abnormally rapid and spontaneous development of the Protestant religion in the region'. This inflammatory language was toned down the following year, after international pressure, and some of its more overtly repressive measures were removed. In 2008, the language was softened further, and the manual now appears to apply to the whole country. It explicitly recognizes that 'religion is a need and will remain a need of some citizens as we build a socialist country,' and religious beliefs must be respected. In 2004, the Vietnamese Prime Minister gave instructions to authorities to 'raise public awareness about the need to create favourable conditions' for churches to worship 'in conformity with the law'.

Nevertheless, despite some improvements, Christians – particularly in the Northern and Central Highlands – continue to suffer restrictions and, in some cases, violent persecution. The training manual for officials dealing with religious affairs still includes a provision to 'encourage ethnic minorities to return to their traditional beliefs if they have a need to do so,' opening the way for arbitrary implementation and inherent discrimination against ethnic minorities who convert to Christianity.

Registration

The key challenge for Christians is the question of registration. While more churches have been able to register their meeting places with the authorities, particularly those associated with the recognized Evangelical Church of Vietnam–North (ECVN-N) and the Evangelical Church of Vietnam–South (ECVN-S), the majority remain unregistered. Even in the ECVN-N, of its 1,000 meeting places, at least 800 had been unable to register in 2009.

The criteria for registration are onerous and prohibitive. For denominations to be legally recognized, they must prove twenty years' 'stable operation', effectively forcing them to operate illegally for twenty years. Individual churches are given provision within the law to register their congregations and meeting places. Prior to Vietnam joining the World Trade Organisation in 2006, the world's eyes were watching the country's religious freedom record, and as a result there was a surge of registrations. However, the process has slowed considerably since this time. Those who remain unregistered can be vulnerable to harassment or threat of closure.

Many applications for registration of meeting places receive no reply, putting the status of churches into legal limbo. Others are rejected by hard-line local officials. In one area, local officials told an applicant bluntly, and wrongly: 'Believing in Christ is illegal under our law so we cannot recognize you', while another was told: 'We don't allow Protestants in this area'. In yet another case, local officials told a church leader: 'Protestantism is anti-Communist and an American religion. If you continue to worship we will imprison you.'

Secret documents reveal true heart

Such attitudes are reflected in leaked secret government documents. These confirm that while a veneer of religious freedom is being created, to improve Vietnam's international image, the heart of the Communist government has not changed. These secret documents express official concern about the explosive growth of Christianity among the ethnic minorities, and give clear instructions to 'forbid and stop the contagious spread of Protestantism'. A document issued in 1998, entitled 'The Problem of the Enemy Exploiting Religion', reportedly remains in use today.

In 2004 and 2005, two documents were issued by the Vietnamese government to establish the framework for religious activities. In some ways, they are an improvement. The 'Ordinance Regarding Religious Beliefs and Religious Organizations', and the 'Decree on Religion', guarantee freedom of religion and belief, and prohibit religious discrimination. However, vague wording in some clauses continues to create problems for Christians. Articles prohibiting the 'abuse' of religion to undermine national unity, to 'sow division' or to 'spread superstitious practices' are wide open to misinterpretation and misuse.

Forced renunciations and familial pressure

A new tactic increasingly used by local officials involves the incitement of family members to pressure converts to Christianity to renounce their faith. Sometimes, this involves domestic violence. One woman who became a Christian in 1997 was beaten so severely by her husband, after she refused to renounce her faith and participate in ancestor worship, that she was unable to walk. Her husband reported her to the police and urged them to imprison her. When she complained to the district-level women's organization about the domestic violence, she was told they could not help her and she should obey her husband. They added that if his violence had been for any other reason, they would intervene, but because it was due to her religious beliefs, they could not help. They urged her to renounce her faith.

Violence and imprisonment

In some cases, Christian pastors are physically assaulted by the Vietnamese authorities. On 17 February 2009, for example, local officials came to a Baptist Church in Hung Yen province and disrupted the Sunday service. They told the church they could not continue to worship unless they submitted an application for permission. The church submitted an application, which was immediately refused.

Two months later, the pastor was stopped 200 metres from the church meeting place, by two plain-clothed police on motorbikes. They pushed his motorbike to the ground and beat him in his face.

On 31 May, a group of twenty plain-clothed officers came to the church meeting place, took the pastor's Bible away, and held his neck so he was unable to speak. Two men held his arms behind his back and took him out of the house, where his shirt was ripped off and he was beaten about the head and shoulders. He was told by the police that he would be imprisoned and then expelled from the area, and was asked to sign papers confirming this. He refused to sign, and was eventually released.

Further attacks continued for several months, and on 21 June 2009 the pastor was again taken to the People's Committee office, along with three members of his congregation. He was held in a small room, where five men beat him with a chair, a fan and their shoes and then with rods and an electric baton. His wife, held in another room, heard his screams and came to the room but the guards held her back and banged her head against the door, causing her to lose consciousness. An hour later, the pastor was beaten again, before being released. His wife, who was by now unable to walk, was accused by police of playing games and her head was bashed against the wall again. She lost consciousness a second time, and was carried out and thrown in a field near another village.

In May 2003, the Vietnamese authorities arrested Pastor Than Van Truong, and imprisoned him without charge for nine months. A former Vietnamese People's Army officer, Pastor Truong became a Christian and eventually a pastor in the Baptist General Conference house church movement. His troubles began when he sent Bibles to Vietnam's top leaders with a message encouraging them to consult the Scriptures for truth and wisdom. That led to his arrest, and after his release he was kept under close surveillance. In June 2004, he was re-arrested. In one of the most flagrant injustices in Vietnam's recent history, the Dong Nai Province authorities diagnosed Pastor Truong as 'delusional' and had him committed to a high security section of the Bien Hoa Mental Hospital on 30 September 2004. While there he was injected with unknown drugs and became ill and lethargic. He was moved to a wing of the hospital which contained genuine psychiatric patients, some of whom attacked him. No criminal charges were made against Pastor Truong, and a sympathetic doctor told his wife he showed no sign of mental disorder.

In the mental hospital, however, he shared his faith with his fellow patients and even baptized some of them. In April 2005 he was released, and has resumed his ministry. The authorities have refused to issue him with a passport, or to give him a registration certificate for his house, and have urged his neighbours not to associate with him. Sometimes the local officials incite people to stone his house. Despite all this, Pastor Truong is continuing to preach and minister to his community.

Conclusion

Whether brutal and violent or subtle and restrictive, the Vietnamese Communist authorities have been unable to stop the growth of the Church. Christians such as Pastor Nguyen are testament to this. He grew up in a proud Communist family. His parents wore the medals they had received from the party for good service, and when he became a Christian they reacted with fury. His brothers refused to speak to him and his parents told the local People's Committee they had disowned him. He said wistfully: 'They were very sad about me. They thought someone paid or bribed me to do this and that I was very stupid.'

Pastor Nguyen was forced to move away from his hometown. He moved with his family to another location, where they started a church in their home. However, government opposition was so strong it was almost impossible to worship other than early in the morning. For a year, from 2002–2003, the pastor and a small group of believers met secretly from 4–5 a.m. to read the Bible, study and quietly pray. Singing was impossible. In 2006, Pastor Nguyen was arrested and interrogated for three days. He had been found visiting local villages, and was accused of distributing illegal materials and being involved in 'illegal evangelism'. The pastor fasted and prayed throughout his three-day ordeal and eventually, after being taken to the district police office, he was released and allowed to return home.

Since then, Pastor Nguyen's church has grown in strength, confidence and numbers, and the authorities appear to have softened in their attitude towards him. He has erected a cross over the gate of the church, which he staunchly refuses to remove. His steadfast faith has been rewarded. Despite their intransigent and furious opposition to his conversion, his own family have seen what his faith means. His mother, initially so hostile, has become a Christian, and before his death, his father stood up at a public meeting and made the following declaration:

> My son follows a religion that I don't know much about. But one thing I know, before, he was a gangster, he beat people and no one would stand up to him because they knew his family were Communist Party members; but now, he is a good man. Only religion can do that. The Party and the government cannot make a man like that.

In the little church in Cu Hat, similar faith has resulted in new life. The pregnant mother who was beaten by the police with an electric cattle prod gave birth to a healthy baby, despite fears of a miscarriage. And three days after their church was destroyed, the community rebuilt it. It is not as beautiful as the original, and with a simple roof made of thin tarpaulin it will be wet in the rainy season, but it stands as a symbol of their courageous, resilient and tenacious faith.

Epilogue
The Stones Cry Out

Jonathan Aitken

The image of stones crying out evokes a discordant, disturbing and almost revolutionary cacophony. Perhaps that was what Jesus intended when he spoke these strange words when entering Jerusalem on his way to the Cross. The context of his prophesy, as recounted in Luke's gospel, becomes even more unsettling with its references to encircling enemies who 'will dash you to the ground, you and the children within your walls. They will not leave one stone on another because you did not recognise the time of God's coming to you' (Lk. 19.40–45)

How like the pain of the persecuted Church this sounds! And how unlike the venerable stones of the established churches whose magnificent naves, pillars, arches, flying buttresses and east windows exude a solidity which too often conceals their spiritual aridity.

Yet judgements based on ecclesiastical exteriors should be avoided, otherwise one falls into the trap set by the paradox of Oscar Wilde: 'It is only shallow people who do not judge by appearances.' Pondering on my own spiritual journey, which has moved forward in an extraordinary variety of surroundings, it seems that prayers for the persecuted Church can be answered in both the most beautiful and the most banal of settings.

As I write this Epilogue I am looking at the notebook given to me by the school chaplain who prepared me for confirmation. He was The Reverend Basil Greenup, who occasionally preached to us schoolboys about the plight of Christians he had visited behind the Iron Curtain. I recall his concerns not because of my brilliant memory for sermons delivered in Eton College Chapel some fifty-four years ago but because I still have the notes I took on them at that time. As part of the confirmation class preparations we were required to make these notes and to draw up a schedule of subjects for daily prayer.

On Tuesdays, our notebooks suggested that we should pray for 'The Church in all lands where Christians have to face persecution'. On the opposite page there are blank spaces with titles such as: Names of countries; Type of Suffering; and Freedom Fighters.

In my teenage handwriting I filled in the empty slots in these ways: Iron Curtain countries, especially Hungary; Poland; Ukraine; Russia.

Their type of suffering was: persecution, particularly the bombardment of churches by Soviet tanks during the Hungarian uprising of 1956.

My freedom fighter selected for prayer was: Father T. Huddleston.

I consider it a minor miracle that my confirmation notebook should have survived for more than five decades. But the major miracle is that the Church is no longer persecuted in any of the countries prayed for. The Iron Curtain has fallen. The spiritual battle against apartheid, so bravely fought by Trevor Huddleston and other Christian leaders, has been won. Faith flourishes freely today in Hungary, Ukraine, Poland, Russia and most other former Communist countries. These victories would have sounded almost unimaginable to the boys who were confirmed at Eton on 22 March 1958. Perhaps we should have listened more carefully to the prayer of our founder King Henry VI: 'O Lord thou hath made us, redeemed us, and brought us to the place where now we are. Thou knowest what thou wilt do with us. Deal with us according to thy will with mercy.'

God does indeed deal mercifully with his faithful followers. His will is for us to say prayers and take actions in his name. But in our enfeebled English churches there are not nearly enough of these activities dedicated to our brothers and sisters suffering from persecution. Yet their need has never been greater because around the world in the twenty-first century the human rights of Christians are being violated on a wider scale than ever before in recorded history.

Five years ago I became Honorary President of Christian Solidarity Worldwide (CSW), succeeding (most inadequately!) Caroline Cox and working with many talented advocates she had inspired, including Ben Rogers.

CSW works at the sharp end of supporting the persecuted Church. We have our frustrations and failures, but also our joyful successes. For the latter we give the glory to God. But to give one example of how our effort follows his will, the recent release of Aung San Suu Kyi from captivity in Burma surely owes much to the tireless campaigning and writing of Ben Rogers during CSW's long campaign to expose the appalling human rights record of that country's military leadership over many years.

There are no quick fixes in advocacy for the plight of the persecuted Church. It is a long haul effort which needs committed faith and works. Yet the Lord clearly listens to those who focus part of their daily prayers on his suffering servants. The story of my Eton confirmation notebook is one long-term example of this. Here is a second personal anecdote in which the short-term results of prayer were much quicker. In 2001 I visited China as a member of a CSW delegation to churches which were being persecuted there. At that time the attitude of the PRC government was oppressive to gatherings of believers who were not authorized by officialdom. I have never forgotten the atmosphere of fear when our delegation, under cover of darkness, made a rendezvous with a group of young Christians at their weekly Bible study session. We climbed some nine storeys of a tower block in a run-down district of Beijing. When we reached the tiny apartment of the group leader we found it jam-packed with students reading Luke's Gospel. Their pastor explained the pressures of harassment (or worse) which these young believers had to endure if they were caught practising their faith.

The pastor's name was Paul Zhiyong. He was a former

corporate lawyer who had turned away from the big bucks and big deals of his successful legal practice in order to become the assistant minister of an underground church. The burning zeal of his faith, his mastery of the English language and his interest in reformed theology made him a kindred spirit to me. At that time I was studying theology at Wycliffe Hall Oxford, so I bonded with Pastor Paul Zhiyong during the six days of our CSW visit.

When I was leaving Beijing for the flight back to London, I had an emotional and prayerful leave-taking from Paul at the airport. He said to me: 'You are so lucky being able to study theology at Oxford under famous professors like Alister McGrath; to work in libraries full of books and to go on missions led by great pastors like Michael Green. Here in Beijing the teachers are very old and out of date. We are desperately short of books. Studying theology is a struggle.'

I responded to Pastor Paul's cri de coeur with a spur of the moment suggestion whose chances of working must have been at least 500:1 against. For I said to my guide and interpreter who had become my friend: 'If Wycliffe was able to find a place for you could you come to Oxford to study theology?' At first Paul Zhiyong's face lit up with excitement but within seconds his expression crumpled into disappointment. 'There is nothing more I would like to do,' he replied, 'but it would not be possible. My church has only just taken me on as an assistant pastor and they could not spare me. The authorities would not give me a travel visa. And I think I could not possibly raise the funds.'

These obstacles sounded insuperable, but we parted agreeing to say prayers for the possibility of Paul coming to Oxford. When I returned to Wycliffe a group of us started to pray for it. Then small miracles began happening. Our Principal, Professor Alister McGrath, offered a subsidized place to the college's first-ever potential theology student from China. The underground church in Beijing agreed to release Paul from his pastoral duties. CSW raised the money to pay his costs. The authorities, amazingly, gave him an exit visa. Less than six weeks after our airport parting I was welcoming

Paul Zhiyong at Heathrow as a theology student of Oxford University.

The semester Paul spent at Wycliffe was important to his own spiritual and theological development. It was also inspirational to the college and to many churches in and around Oxford. For a few weeks, Zhiyong and Aitken were a double-bill of Christian speakers on the persecuted Church. He far outshone me in eloquence and erudition but between us we made an impact. With the help of CSW, Wycliffe and several church leaders, a real surge of enthusiasm took place about praying for the plight of beleaguered Christians in China. Since the number of those Christians has grown from approximately 30 million to well over 100 million in the past ten years and since the persecution of them, although not yet over, has eased considerably, those prayers seem to have been well answered.

In my heady days of travelling around Oxford as Pastor Paul Zhiyong's warm-up man, I used to think that engaging churches in the UK about commitment to and solidarity with the persecuted Church was an easy task. Now I know better. It is an uphill struggle. I concur with the pessimistic view expressed in the Foreword of this book which stated that in their attitudes to the persecuted church 'a significant proportion of congregations in the West are still unaware, uninformed and unengaged'.

Why does this apathy prevail? It is not because church attendance figures are down (which in many parts of the country they are not – for example in the Diocese of London where the annual number of communicants has been rising by 3 per cent or more for the past five years). Nor is it because committed Christians are less interested in their faith. There are ample signs from the warm public response to the Pope's visit, to the record-breaking number of Anglican ordinations, and to the growth of Alpha courses which suggest that spiritual hunger is a real feature of our national life.

Yet despite all sorts of indications that the body of Christ may be in better health in twenty-first century Britain than detractors of the Church allege, the uncomfortable fact remains that certain 'difficult' ministries are poorly supported from the pews.

Take Christian prison ministry, which is increasingly being marginalized by multi-faith compromises, pressure from Imams and political correctness in Whitehall. Some five years ago Holy Trinity Brompton wrote to all its 7,200 Alpha churches inviting them to participate in a new ministry of prayer and rehabilitation – Caring for Ex Offenders. Only 700 of those churches responded, which means that 90 per cent of them, like the priest in the parable of the Good Samaritan 'passed by on the other side'.

Some might argue that to get 10 per cent of our churches actively involved in the challenging work of caring for ex-offenders or helping victims of religious persecution (alas another minority interest among most of the faithful) is not a bad score. But the teachings of Jesus, notably the parable of the sheep and the goats (Matthew 25.31–46) suggest that his followers should give far higher priority to what he called 'the least of these my brethren'.

This is not a new problem. Seven centuries ago the author of what is still the best selling book of Christian literature after the Bible, Thomas à Kempis, wrote in *The Imitation of Christ*:

Jesus has many lovers of his heavenly Kingdom but few bearers of his Cross. He has many followers who desire consolation but few who accept tribulation. All desire to rejoice with him but few to suffer for his sake. Many accompany Jesus to the breaking of the bread but few are willing to drink the cup of his passion.

Behind the medieval language lies a modern reality. Church life today is too often inward looking, congenial, consoling, comfortable and lacking in passion. Too rarely does it move outwards to fight the good fight in the arenas where perse-cution and the violation of Christian human rights is a daily battle.

So what's to be done? The anecdote about my confirmation class notebook perhaps offers some glimmering of hope. In the 1950s, saying prayers for the fall of communism and apartheid may have felt discouraging. Today the plight of the various oppressed Christian communities highlighted by the chapters of this book may seem a difficult cause to champion. But God is in charge. His timing may not be in accord with the cycles of power and politics. Yet we can be sure that he will show mercy and compassion to his suffering servants. For the eighth beatitude 'Blessed are those who are persecuted' (Mt. 5.10) is his promise, even though the stones continue to cry out on the way to the fulfilment of it.

Footnote on Terminology

The word 'Catholic' is used in several ways and in different contexts.

For example, it is used in major formulations of the Christian Creed, including the Nicene Creed and the Apostles' Creed. Christians who belong to denominations which affirm such creeds thereby declare themselves as members of the 'Catholic Church'.

Various denominations specifically include the word 'Catholic' in their determining identities. The Roman Catholic Church is the largest; other specifically named 'Catholic' churches include the 'Anglo-Catholic' part of the Anglican Church; the 'Armenian Catholic Church' and the 'Assyrian Catholic Church'.

However, given the global nature of the Roman Catholic Church and the everyday use of the word 'Catholic' typically to refer to this part of the overall Christian church, we will generally follow this traditional terminology, using the word 'Catholic' to refer to the Roman Catholic Church.

Notes

Chapter 1

1 Benedict Rogers, *Carrying the Cross: The Military Regime's Campaign of Restriction, Discrimination and Persecution Against Christians in Burma*, (Christian Solidarity Worldwide, 2007), p. 3.
2 Ibid., p. 17.
3 *CSW Condemns Crackdown on Churches in Rangoon*, (Christian Solidarity Worldwide) 15 January 2009.
4 Ibid.
5 Ibid.
6 Benedict Rogers, *Carrying the Cross: The Military Regime's Campaign of Restriction, Discrimination and Persecution Against Christians in Burma*, (Christian Solidarity Worldwide, 2007), p. 17.
7 Ibid., p. 3.

Chapter 5

1 David Schenker, '*Renewed Violence against Egypt's Coptic Christians*', (The Washington Institute for Near Eastern Studies), 15 January 2010.
2 See CSW Briefing 'Egypt' August 2007.
3 Paul Marshall 'Apostates from Islam: The Case of the Afghan Convert is not Unique', The *Weekly Standard*, 2 April 2006.
4 ILO Global Report: 'Taking the Challenge', 2007.
5 'Persecuted and Forgotten? A Report on Christians Oppressed for their Faith', 2007/8', p.36, Aid to the Church in Need.
6 info@the-candle.com.

Chapter 6

1 *India:Communalism, Anti-Christian Violence and the Law*, (Christian Solidarity Worldwide, May 2010).
2 For a report of our findings, including interviews with many of the victims, see Report of HART Visit to Orissa, India, 30 October–4 November 2008, available from Humanitarian Aid Relief Trust, www.hart-uk.org.

Chapter 7

1 See *Cox's Book of Modern Saints and Martyrs*, Caroline Cox with Catherine Butcher, Continuum, Chapter 1, 2006, reprinted 2007, 2008 and 2009.
2 See CSW Briefing: Indonesia Visit report, 10–23 July 2010.

Notes

3 *Wall Street Journal.*

4 See CSW Briefing: Indonesia Visit report, July 2010.

5 CSW Briefing: Indonesia Visit report, July 2010.

6 For an account of subsequent developments after Reverend Damanik's trial, see *Cox's Book of Modern Saints and Martyrs'*, ibid.

7 ?

Chapter 8

1 See http://www.elam.com/articles/Maryam-and-Marzieh--Acquitted-and-Free for a full account of their story.

2 For a detailed history of these denominations see Mark Bradley's *Iran and Christianity Part 2*, (London: Continuum). After the decline of Spain and Portugal, the Roman Catholics never had a strong presence in Iran.

3 See Mark Bradley's *Iran and Christianity* Chapter 9, (London: Continuum, 2008), p.164.

4 'Dhimmitude' comes from the Arabic word 'dhimmi' which means protected. The word was first used by Bat Ye'or, historian of the Eastern Church, to describe the status of Christians and Jews in the Muslim state.

5 See Mark Bradley's *Iran and Christianity Part One*, (London: Continuum) for a full discussion of Iran's historical identity.

6 This author knows a European who asked a Revolutionary Guard whether Iran executes apostates from Islam. The guard shook his head vigorously in denial. Though he was later contradicted by his senior, this illustrates the general lack of enthusiasm for killing apostates.

7 See www.elam.com for more information about this important support ministry for the Church in Iran. In the last few years this agency has sent nearly half a million New Testaments to Iran.

8 In October 1979 an attempt was also made on the life of the then leader of the Anglican Church, the late Bishop Hasan Dehqani-Tafti. Two armed men broke into his flat in the early hours and fired shots at the sleeping bishop and his wife, Margaret. They missed. Sadly the bishop's eldest son was not so fortunate. He was abducted and murdered in May 1980.

9 The full story of Bishop Haik Hovsepian's martyrdom is told in the moving documentary 'Cry From Iran' produced by his sons, Joseph and Gilbert.

10 For more detail on Iran's poets and Jesus Christ see Mark Bradley's *Iran and Christianity*, (London: Continuum), Chapter 2.

11 Elam Ministries, one the largest agencies serving the Church in Iran, has a free prayer guide, 'Iran 30' which is available from the website, www.iran30.org or their offices in the UK and USA.

Chapter 9

1 Nina Shea, 'Iraq's Christians Still Under Siege', NRO Corner Blog, 1 November 2010 http://crf.hudson.org/index.cfm?fuseaction=publication_details&id=7476&pubType=CRF_Opeds

Notes

Chapter 10
1 Information provided by Christian Solidarity Worldwide.
2 Release International.
3 BosNewsLife Asia Service – http://www.christianpersecution.info/news/laos-threatens-expulsion-christian-villagers-widow-forgives-husbands-killers-16425/.

Chapter 11
1 See Caroline Cox and John Eibner, 'Ethnic Cleansing in Progress: The War in Nagorno Karabakh'.

Chapter 12
1 See Report of HART visit to Nigeria, 2008
2 CSW Briefing 26/6/07; Compass Direct News, 2007; ACN 'Persecuted and Forgotten?' 2008.
3 See HART Visit report, March 2009.
4 HART visit report March 2009.
5 HART visit report July 2010.
6 HART visit report, ibid.

Chapter 14
1 Rowan Williams, 'A truly Islamic state would protect Christians,' *The Times*, 7 March 2011.
2 Christian Solidarity Worldwide, 'Pakistani Christians given 10 days to convert to Islam as National Assembly rejects reform of blasphemy laws', 14 May 2007.
3 http://www.bbc.co.uk/news/world-south-asia-12617562.
4 Christian Solidarity Worldwide, 'Massacre in church shows extent of threat to Christian minority in Pakistan', 29 October 2001.
5 Ibid.
6 Christian Solidarity Worldwide, 'Pakistani militants call for elimination of Christians and public hanging of blasphemy prisoner', 12 December 2005.
7 Christian Solidarity Worldwide, 'Catholic girls' school latest casualty of violence in Pakistan', 9 October 2008.
8 Christian Solidarity Worldwide, 'CSW renews call for repeal of blasphemy laws in Pakistan', 30 July 2010.
9 Compass Direct, 'Christians narrowly escape flying bullets in Pakistan', 15 July 2010.
10 Compass Direct, 'Two Pakistan Christian churches come under attack from Islamists', 13 July 2010.
11 Christian Solidarity Worldwide, 'Christians targeted in Pakistan over Easter period; twelve year-old Pakistani girl gang-raped on Easter Day', 27 April 2010.
12 Christian Solidarity Worldwide, 'Visit to Pakistan', October 2004.

Notes

13 Compass Direct, 'Rapes of Christian girls in Pakistan reflect hidden trend', 16 August 2010.

14 Christian Solidarity Worldwide, 'CSW calls on Pakistani authorities to return abducted Christian girls to their family', 31 July 2008.

15 Christian Solidarity Worldwide, 'Pakistan – Alleged kidnapper granted custody of Christian girl', 10 September 2008.

16 Christian Solidarity Worldwide, 'Visit to Pakistan', October 2004.

17 Compass Direct, 'Christians accused of "blasphemy" slain in Pakistan', 19 July 2010.

18 Benedict Rogers, 'Blasphemy laws and the persecution of minorities in Pakistan', Religion Compass, 27 January 2009.

19 Nicola Smith, 'I'll die next: new hero defies Pakistan's blasphemy hardliners', *The Sunday Times*, 6 March 2011.

Chapter 15

1 Special Representative of the Foreign and Commonwealth Office Freedom of Religion Panel, Report on Anti-Conversion Legislation in Sri Lanka, 2005.

2 Special Representative of the Foreign and Commonwealth Office Freedom of Religion Panel, Report on Anti-Conversion Legislation in Sri Lanka, 2005.

3 Christian Solidarity Worldwide, 'Sri Lanka: religious freedom in the post-conflict situation', January 2010.

4 Special Representative of the Foreign and Commonwealth Office Freedom of Religion Panel, Report on Anti-Conversion Legislation in Sri Lanka, 2005.

5 Christian Solidarity Worldwide, 'Fresh violence and threats hit Sri Lankan Christians', 20 February 2006.

6 Christian Solidarity Worldwide, 'Sri Lankan Buddhist extremists attack church-run children's home and threatend death', 10 August 2006.

7 Christian Solidarity Worldwide, 'Sri Lanka: dramatic increase in violence against Christians', 4 March 2008.

8 Christian Solidarity Worldwide, 'Christian girl attacked by fellow students amidst increasing opposition to Sri Lanka's Christians', 19 June 2008.

9 Christian Solidarity Worldwide, 'Sri Lanka: Religious freedom in the post-conflict situation', January 2010.

10 Special Representative of the Foreign and Commonwealth Office Freedom of Religion Panel, Report on Anti-Conversion Legislation in Sri Lanka, 2005.

11 Special Representative of the Foreign and Commonwealth Office Freedom of Religion Panel, Report on Anti-Conversion Legislation in Sri Lanka, 2005.

12 Special Representative of the Foreign and Commonwealth Office

Notes

Freedom of Religion Panel, Report on Anti-Conversion Legislation in Sri Lanka, 2005.

13 Christian Solidarity Worldwide, 'Sri Lanka: dramatic Increase in violence against Christians', 4 March 2008.

14 Christian Solidarity Worldwide, 'Sri Lanka: religious freedom in the post-conflict situation', January 2010.

Chapter 16

1 See Caroline Cox and John Marks, 'This immoral trade: slavery in the 21st century'.

2 Aid to the Church in Need 'Persecuted or Forgotten?' 2008, p. 91.